You Can't Live in the Ceilings

*Practical Advice for Home Buyers, Sellers,
and the Agents Who Serve Them*

MARY CLEAVER

◆ FriesenPress

One Printers Way
Altona, MB R0G 0B0
Canada

www.friesenpress.com

http://marycleaver.com

ISBN
978-1-03-832665-2 (Hardcover)
978-1-03-832664-5 (Paperback)
978-1-03-832666-9 (eBook)

I. BUSINESS & ECONOMICS, REAL ESTATE, BUYING & SELLING HOMES

Distributed to the trade by The Ingram Book Company

TABLE OF CONTENTS

Introduction

Many years before I became a REALTOR®, I was looking to buy my first home in Vancouver. I had been living with a roommate who was also a close friend, and the two of us planned to move in with my boyfriend (now my husband). We were hunting for a two-bedroom condo – ideally in the Kitsilano or Fairview neighbourhoods.

One day, we came across a top-floor apartment with gorgeous, vaulted ceilings. I fell in love on the spot. My boyfriend and roommate, however, were convinced that at 750 square feet, the condo was too cosy for the three of us. I remained undeterred. Did I mention I was *in love*? My realtor listened patiently as we debated the pros and cons. When there was a break in the conversation, he looked me straight in the eyes. "You can't live in the ceilings, Mary," he said, with a smile. Those seven words changed everything. I left the condo without any regrets.

Soon after, we found a two-bedroom-and-den in the same area. It was a little over 1,100 square feet with a smart layout and two full bathrooms; perfect for three people. It wasn't quite as pretty, but the extra square footage enabled us to live there comfortably for six years. By the time my husband and I needed more space, we had built the equity we needed to buy our next home.

As I think back, I marvel that my realtor's opinion – rather than what my close friend and boyfriend had to say – so quickly convinced me to reconsider the condo. His wise counsel carried me through a few key real estate decisions over the years and, eventually, inspired me to become a realtor, too. I'm keenly aware that many of my clients trust me the way I trusted Dale; helping people with these consequential decisions is an awesome responsibility.

However, most people don't enjoy the process so much that they become licensed realtors. Rather, they operate between two ends of the spectrum:

1. **The Keeners:** They visit REALTOR.ca at least once a day, consume videos and podcasts about real estate, rattle off market stats and interest rates, and spend the weekend hitting up open houses – just for fun. Keeners ask a lot of questions, use their own judgement, offer suggestions, and are more prepared than a Broadway cast on opening night. In short, they're totally engaged and enjoy the experience.

2. **The Transactionals:** These people want to get in, get out, and move on. They don't want to know the finer points of real estate. After all, they lead busy lives and have their own jobs, *thank you very much*. Transactionals aren't terribly interested in why we choose one marketing strategy over another, and they're happy to take my lead on most decisions. "What do you think I should do?" is a common refrain. They've hired me to do a job, and they trust me to do it well.

When you think of your own experiences with buying or selling a home, where do you fall on the spectrum? Are you excited to play an active role? Are you totally hands off? Or do you land somewhere in between?

Why your participation matters

People who engage meaningfully with their agents become valuable partners in the process. Most importantly, they tend to get better results: a more suitable home, a better deal, a more enjoyable experience, or all of the above. After all, your realtor is the expert on markets, negotiation, valuations, promotion, document review, and writing an enforceable contract, but *you* are the expert on your home, neighbourhood, financial means, motivation, lifestyle, and your plans for the future. Together, you're a powerful team.

This book tells you what you can expect from the most service-oriented, highly skilled real estate practitioners and teams. You'll learn:

- How realtors get paid
- The legal duties they owe to you
- How timing and preparation can increase a home's value
- Marketing and pricing strategies
- Practical considerations when buying or selling
- What your agent needs from you to negotiate for the best possible outcome
- And more

Knowing how the industry works empowers you to choose the right realtor, collaborate effectively, and hold them accountable throughout the process.

Read this book from cover to cover for a good foundation, or refer to certain sections when you're thinking about buying or selling – or if you're right in the thick of it. You can also use some of the ideas and strategies to have more meaningful conversations and build trust with your realtor.

The agency relationship and real estate fees

This section explores the relationship you'll form with your realtor as you buy or sell a home. We'll cover the duties your realtor owes to you, as legislated by the B.C. Financial Services Authority. We'll discuss how agents are paid and how much, and the variety of services covered within that fee. You'll also find a step-by-step guide to choosing the right agent and some helpful suggestions to build a trusting relationship.

Note:

Real estate licensees have passed the licensing exam and can practice real estate in B.C. Realtors® are members of the national, provincial, and local real estate organizations and must adhere to the rules and code of conduct of these associations. The vast majority of licensees are realtors, and for that reason, we'll refer to these professionals as either agents or realtors throughout this book.

CHAPTER 1:
THE REAL ESTATE AGENT'S ROLE

Understanding an agent's role can help you decide whether to enter into a relationship with a realtor. Knowing how you're protected within that relationship can make you feel more comfortable sharing information, because your agent uses these details for your benefit and maintains full confidentiality during and after the transaction.

If you choose to interact with a realtor who's not your agent, it's important to understand that you're not owed a duty of care, so you can't expect confidentiality and other protections in that circumstance.

In this chapter, we'll cover:

- Why consumers hire agents rather than selling or buying on their own

- The agent's legal duties when working on behalf of a client

- When you might interact with realtors who aren't your agent

- How a customer relationship with an agent differs from working within the agency relationship

You can certainly buy and sell a home without a realtor. But, the vast majority of buyers and sellers choose to hire one for several reasons:

The stakes are high – for sellers and buyers

Your home may be your largest financial investment, and it's probably a big part of your net worth. That means selling your home is a high-stakes endeavour. Simply put, there's a lot of money on the table – and while no one loves paying real estate fees, an experienced team with outstanding negotiation skills can lead to a smoother process and a higher sale price. Saving the fee could ultimately cost you a lot of money, to say nothing of the considerable time and emotional toll it would take to list your own home.

Buyers are also in a risky position. A skilled and dedicated agent or team will help you evaluate the quality and suitability of a property, negotiate for the best price, navigate a multiple offer situation, and help you make the right choice for your family and your financial future.

You receive legal benefits

Just like lawyers, notaries, and other professionals, B.C. real estate agents fulfil what's known as a fiduciary role. That means your agent has four legal duties:

1. Loyalty

2. Full disclosure

3. Avoid conflicts of interest

4. Confidentiality

Loyalty, full disclosure of relevant information, and avoiding conflicts of interest are necessary throughout the buying or selling process, and those duties end when the transaction is complete. The requirement to keep a client's personal information confidential lasts forever.

In B.C., the realtor's legal duties are disclosed to consumers in a legislated form called "The Disclosure of Representation in Trading

Services," which you'll find in the accompanying Resource Guide, available for download at marycleaver.com/resourceguide. When you interact with a realtor outside of the agency relationship, agents have a responsibility to act with honesty and reasonable care and skill, but they don't have those four legal duties.

For example, you might chat with a realtor who's not your agent at an open house, on the phone, or when you send or receive an email about a listing you find online. In these circumstances, and in the rare instances when you choose to list or buy a home without hiring an agent, you may interact with agents outside of a signed agency relationship.

Whatever the reason, remember that this agent only owes you honesty and reasonable care and skill – but not loyalty, confidentiality, full disclosure, or a duty to avoid conflicts of interest. In most cases, the agent will be working for another party, and owes those duties to *their* client. Proceed with caution. Be careful not to share your personal information; the realtor could use that information to benefit their client, which they're not only allowed to do, but legally *required to do* in certain circumstances.

Imagine it's Saturday afternoon and you notice an open house sign in your desired neighbourhood. The house smells like chocolate chip cookies and the listing realtor is just *so nice*. She's warm and chatty. Between sips of coffee, you confide that your child hopes to enrol in the school down the street, so your family is eager to buy in this catchment. Eventually, you make an offer. The listing realtor remembers you and advises the seller to stay firm on their price; she knows you're eager and motivated. That short, casual conversation may have cost you tens of thousands of dollars.

Now that you understand why you might want to hire a professional to help with your real estate purchase or sale, and you understand the realtor's legal duties, let's learn how they get paid.

CHAPTER 2:
HOW AGENTS GET PAID, AND THE
ROLE OF THE AGENT'S BROKERAGE

M̲ost realtors don't work for companies and they're not employees. Let's talk about how the real estate industry functions, specifically:

- The structure and responsibilities within a British Columbia real estate brokerage, including the role of the managing broker, and payment arrangements for listing and buyer's agents

- Why it's important for buyers and sellers to know how realtors are compensated

- The most common compensation structure for realtors in British Columbia

B.C. agents are required to be licensed within a brokerage, led by a managing broker who has a different real estate licence than their agents. The managing broker oversees the realtors and is responsible for ensuring agents carry out their duties, that deposit funds are properly held and accounted for, and that information is disclosed and gathered as required by governing bodies.

Both the listing agent and the agent working on behalf of the buyer are typically paid by the seller, so neither party has to pay their realtor until the transaction is complete. The fee is negotiable, and it's agreed to by the agent and the seller in a contract they both sign before a property is marketed for sale, referred to as the listing agreement. The agreed-upon fee is shared between both agents and pulled from the proceeds of the real estate transaction.

How do agents get paid?

First, you need to know that real estate fees are negotiable. Most B.C. markets, certainly in Vancouver and throughout the Lower Mainland, are home to a variety of realtors competing for your business. Throughout this book, whenever I talk about realtors, I'm referring to those who work with full-service agencies, rather than discount brokerages, auction houses, or For Sale By Owner packages available online. These models represent an extremely small number of transactions in the Lower Mainland.

In the vast majority of transactions, both realtors are paid by the seller from the proceeds of a property sale. At no point will you be asked to pay your realtor directly, such as by charging a fee on your credit card. Remember: agents only get paid when you've successfully bought or sold a home.

Why does the seller pay both agents if the buyer's agent works exclusively for the buyer?

Great question. It does seem counterintuitive for the seller to pay an agent to negotiate for another party. This arrangement is typical in both the U.S. and Canada, but not in many other parts of the world. Buyer agency wasn't originally part of our industry, meaning that listing agents signed agreements with sellers, and many buyers didn't have an agent at all.

Over time, it became clear that buyers needed representation to protect their interests in these large transactions. Perhaps it was a competitive advantage or simply expedient for seller's agents to "cooperate" with the other side, in terms of splitting the fee, as opposed to a system where buyers paid their agents directly.

As the seller, you *can* decide not to offer a co-operating commission to the buyer's agent. That's completely within your rights, but it could affect a buyer's motivation to purchase your home, because they'd have to pay their agent out of pocket. Few sellers go this route, perhaps because they remember the same arrangement when they bought their home, and if they're also buying a home, they know they won't have to pay their agent on the buying side. The convenience of this arrangement seems to work well for both sides.

When you know how realtors are compensated and you understand the typical fee range, you're in a better position to negotiate when meeting prospective agents. If you're selling, the real estate fee is an expense you'll have to account for, along with legal fees and moving costs.

*DID YOU KNOW?

Real estate teams are actually small businesses. Realtors don't work for brokerages, and they don't generally earn a salary. Rather, realtors choose their brokerage and pay dues that cover the cost of the managing broker, administrative staff, trust accounts, office space, and more. Some choose an international brand, such as RE/MAX or Sutton, while others choose local, boutique firms such as Stilhavn and Oakwyn in B.C. Agents may move their business to another brokerage from time to time, but this change shouldn't affect their client service.

How much can a seller expect to pay to list their home with a full-service brokerage?

In B.C., real estate fees are usually expressed as a percentage of the property sale price. Agents are free to set their own prices and negotiate fees with their clients. While there's no legislated or set amount that realtors can charge, it's a highly competitive market; fees generally stay within a certain range and realtors rarely discuss their fees with competitors, for obvious reasons. However, home-owners often share this information with me.

Sometimes they ask me to match an offered price, or they confirm that my fee falls in line with those offered by other agents. On rare occasions, I even get to see a physical copy of another agent's listing presentation. Over the years, I've found that sellers in British Columbia can expect to pay somewhere between 3 and 3.5 per cent of the purchase price of the home, give or take.

Here are some examples of the fees you might expect to pay if you're selling a home for $1 million dollars. I have come across all of these options during my time in the industry.

Option A

7% on the first $100,000 and 3% on the balance
= $7,000 + $27,000 = $34,000

Option B

7% on the first $100,000 and 2.5% on the balance
= $7,000 + $22,500 = $29,500

Option C

3.5% on the purchase price
= $35,000

Option D

3% on the purchase price
= $30,000

*Note that the price difference between A, B, C, and D is relatively modest on a home worth $1 million dollars. If your home is worth significantly more, Option B will produce a much lower fee than the other options. You can try some of these basic calculations to gauge the impact of a higher sale price.

In all of these scenarios, the buyer's agent is typically also paid from this fee. It's not an additional amount. When you sign the listing agreement, your agent will outline how much of their fee will go to the buyer's agent. The amount offered to the buyer's agent is also negotiable and will vary, but it's usually between about 45 and 50 per cent of the total fee.

In Greater Vancouver for example, it's customary for the listing agent to keep a little more than half to account for the hard costs inherent in listing a home, such as photography, video, brochures, measurements, and other expenses.

*DID YOU KNOW?

The U.S. real estate industry has undergone some recent changes, based on a lawsuit settlement regarding how fees are charged and communicated to consumers. The lawsuit alleged that the common practice of sellers paying both the buying and selling agents' fees prevented buyers from negotiating that fee with their realtors.

As part of the settlement, and in an effort to achieve full transparency, the U.S. National Association of Realtors will no longer allow its members to offer a co-operating real estate fee to buyer's agents on the Multiple Listing Service (MLS) system. Home sellers can still offer to pay a buyer's agent fee, but it may be offered to the buyer, rather than a fee paid directly to the buyer's agent. This may seem like a minor distinction, but it makes the buyer, and not the agent, the recipient of the offer. For example, if the buyer negotiates a fee with his realtor, and the seller's offer is greater, the buyer would keep the difference.

We haven't seen these changes In Canada, but it's reasonable to expect that our industry may implement changes to ensure greater transparency. It's worth noting that our practices are significantly different from real estate practices south of the border. In B.C., real estate fees are typically much lower than in the U.S. and we're already required to disclose our fee to our buyers, in writing. Across Canada, many of us already use buyer's agency agreements and negotiate fees with our buyer clients.

My own view is that it's still most convenient for the seller to offer to pay the buyer's agent. It encourages buyers to have their own professional representation, which is vitally important. Since the fee comes from the proceeds of the sale, and is generally included in the buyer's mortgage, neither side has to pay out of pocket. As an industry, we could make buyer's agency agreements mandatory to ensure every buyer understands and agrees to how much their agent will be paid, and by whom, earlier in the process.

Agent's fees vary, and are negotiable, but this gives you a rough idea of what to expect when you're interviewing candidates. Please note that Canadian agents are also required to charge the Goods and Services Tax (GST) on their fee.

Generally speaking, the real estate fee covers most, if not all of the expenses associated with selling a home – with the exception of your legal fees. Your agent pays the administrative and marketing costs which, particularly at the higher end of the price spectrum, may also include cleaning and staging. These value-added elements can significantly affect your ultimate sale price, so if you're keen to negotiate with your chosen agent, consider asking for more service inclusions.

CHAPTER 3:
SELECTING YOUR AGENT

As I write, there are about 26,000 licensed realtors in B.C., and 17,000 in the Lower Mainland alone. How do you find the right agent for your needs? A personal connection is just the start. There are some key skills and attributes your realtor should possess, and some practical steps to consider when choosing who will represent you.

Specifically, we'll discuss:

- Five steps to help you research potential realtors and real estate teams – and why this research is essential

- The biggest mistake buyers make when choosing a realtor

- The three most common mistakes sellers make when choosing a realtor

- The five top attributes your realtor must have to ensure you get the best possible results

- Specific questions to ask a buying or listing realtor

Real estate is a competitive field. Across the industry, you'll find a wide range of skill and service levels. Gathering the information you need to make a thoughtful, educated hiring decision is worth every minute of your time.

There's a common misconception that you should choose an agent based on trust and likeability. You may spend a lot of time with this person, so it's great to feel connected. But, you can like and trust someone who doesn't have the skills to guide you through the complicated and highly consequential process of buying or selling real estate.

Agents sometimes get this wrong, too. I can't tell you how many times I've heard agents, even trainers and team leaders, say "we're not selling a product; we're selling ourselves." Well, not exactly. You don't want to buy your agent. You're choosing the agent who has the skill set and motivation to give you the best possible experience and the best results.

The biggest mistake home buyers make when selecting a realtor

Many consumers, and even some real estate professionals, also believe that selecting a buyer's agent is less consequential than choosing a listing agent. Home sellers often carefully consider their options, perhaps because home sellers pay their agent directly, whereas buyers typically do not. Some buyers don't approach the choice intentionally, and fall into an agency relationship with someone who may or may not have the appropriate experience or skill set.

Here's the biggest mistake buyers often make when selecting an agent: choosing a realtor who doesn't specialize in the location they're buying in. For example, the top realtor in Richmond, B.C. is probably not the best choice for a buyer focused on downtown Vancouver. Why? An out-of-market agent rarely knows:

1. **The quality of the buildings**. They haven't read strata documents for many Vancouver buildings, so they're starting their research at the beginning.

2. **The comparative value of the homes you're viewing.** They haven't viewed many of the recently sold listings, so they're not as well equipped to advise buyers on a home's value compared to an agent who typically works in your target area.

3. **The other local realtors.** When it's time to negotiate an offer, an out-of-market agent is less likely to have an existing relationship with the listing agent, which can be invaluable – especially if the home is highly desirable and you're competing against multiple offers.

I feel so strongly about the specialized knowledge local buyer's agents possess that I hired one myself when I was shopping for a small cabin on the Sunshine Coast. As a licensed B.C. realtor, I could have easily represented myself in the purchase and, in all likelihood, received a commission.

I chose to hire a buyer's agent because I believed his local knowledge would help me understand the value of the homes I was viewing. I also wanted to avoid any risks associated with rural properties. And just as my industry relationships are instrumental in securing the right deals for my clients, I knew that his connections to other local agents would serve me well in negotiating the price for a property.

As it turned out, his counsel proved invaluable in selecting the home and negotiating the offer in competition with another buyer. We secured the property at a price well below what we were willing to pay for it; a result I don't think I could have achieved on my own. For us, the value of his local experience and relationships far outweighed the value of the commission he earned.

Home sellers often make three common mistakes when selecting a realtor:

1. Choosing the agent based on the suggested list price for your home

You can see why it's tempting to pick an agent who gives you a big number, but it's the wrong approach. We'll discuss how skilled agents estimate fair market value in a later chapter, but the market isn't something that agents can control.

A high list price may sound great, but it can quickly backfire if your home doesn't sell in the first several weeks and you have to reduce the price. Instead, working with your realtor to set an aspirational but realistic list price (and a plan to achieve it) is a smarter play – and will likely produce a higher sale price than listing well above market value. You can decide on the pricing strategy together, but the suggested list price shouldn't affect who you choose as your agent.

2. Choosing based on the agent's claim that they, or their office, work with a large pool of buyers who may be interested in your home

Any statement like this is a red flag. The most likely buyer for your home is not currently working with your realtor. As I noted earlier, there are 17,000 licensed agents in the Lower Mainland alone. What are the chances that the most qualified, motivated buyer is currently working with your agent? The entire real estate community, and all of their buyers, will learn your home is for sale when it hits REALTOR.ca. Neither information, nor proximity to buyers, has been the valued currency in real estate since the dawn of the internet.

*DID YOU KNOW?

In B.C., it used to be possible for one agent or team to represent both the buyer and seller in the same transaction. This was called limited dual agency, and it was prohibited by British Columbia in 2018 when regulators rightly determined that representing both sides was an irresolvable conflict. There are rare instances when limited dual agency is permitted. For example, when a market is so sparsely populated that there may not be another agent working there. Clearly, that doesn't apply in the Lower Mainland, or in most parts of B.C., so your listing agent will not be representing your buyer – and that's a good thing.

3. Choosing based solely on who offers the lowest fee for their services

We all like to save money. But just like any professional or service provider you might hire, the cheapest option isn't always the best. When selling a home, you can easily net five, six, or even 10 per cent more money with a well-designed and fully executed strategy. If you're focused on skimming less than one per cent off the top of an agent's fee, you're missing the big picture.

In short, don't focus on fees, list price, the agent's pool of buyers, or even trust and likeability. Forget the splashy bus ads, too. Here's what you're really buying when you choose the agent to represent you in a real estate transaction.

When you select a realtor, you're choosing the person or team you believe will offer you the best experience, and the best outcome. They should have the following five professional skills and attributes:

1. Market knowledge

2. Negotiation skills

3. Strong industry relationships

4. The ability to build and execute strategy

5. Excellent customer service

Your agent earns your trust as they exhibit their skill, care, and service to you during the process. It begins with the first conversation. My goal in this chapter, and throughout the book, is to help you understand why these five points result in a better experience and outcome for you, and how to evaluate candidates and confidently choose your realtor.

Be prepared to spend some time on this stage. It can be tempting to sign with the first realtor who's recommended to you, or whose flyer lands in your mailbox that day – especially if you're busy. Please remember that this is likely the biggest financial decision you'll make until you buy or sell your next home.

The cost of real estate in Vancouver, and increasingly throughout B.C., means that this decision affects more than where you'll live (as if that wasn't consequential enough). Your home may also be the biggest element of your wealth generation, your retirement plan, and your estate plan. It's a big deal, so it's worth all the time you can devote to it. Remember: it's just as important to hire a great buyer's agent as it is to have a great listing agent – and the process for selecting this professional service is the same whether you're buying, selling, or both.

Here are five steps you can take to evaluate and ultimately choose your real estate professional:

1. Shortlist four or five agents

Begin by asking friends and family who have recently bought or sold in your neighbourhood to share their experiences. When people love their realtor, they'll tell you! They'll also tell you when they had a less-than-ideal experience. A personal recommendation is the single best way to begin your search for a realtor. If someone you know was well served by a member of our profession, that's a great start.

Compare that to calling a realtor who stuffs your mailbox with their monthly flyers. Advertising doesn't equal skill; it just proves that the agent hired a company to produce content and distribute it by mail. What about agents who appear near the top of your web search? That simply proves the agent invested their resources in Search Engine Optimization (SEO) services and they rely heavily on internet marketing to attract clients.

Recommendations from colleagues, family members, friends, or neighbours are typically far more reliable indicators that someone has the skills you need. If no one in your social circle raves about their agent, you might try to find a personal recommendation through social media. For example, post a note asking for recommendations on a neighbourhood Facebook group. You'll often see the same agent or team pop up more than once, or other people will second a recommendation. That's a good sign.

2. Check online reviews

Once you have a handful of names, look for independent reviews on digital platforms such as Google Reviews or RankMyAgent. These websites are trustworthy because companies can't control what people post. In contrast, a review that appears on an agent's website can be removed or edited. I know this from personal experience.

Years ago, someone posted a poor Google review of my team. The poster wasn't our client, so I tried (but failed) to have it removed. Our only option was to continue providing excellent client service so that over time, the one bad review moved down the list and no longer affected our five-star rating.

As you read several of the reviews, a clear picture should emerge. You'll likely see recurring themes such as personalized service, excellent negotiation skills, good advice, responsive communication, strong industry knowledge, expert strategies, great results, and more. You'll get a sense of where an agent and their team specialize, whether they serve both buyers and sellers with equal dedication, and how consistently and enthusiastically clients rave about them.

3. Select two or three agents for a personal interview

Each meeting will take at least an hour, and likely about 90 minutes, so be selective about who you choose to interview. Don't bother meeting with agents who probably don't fit your needs. Before investing your valuable time, create a short set of criteria and ensure your potential candidates meet those standards.

How to choose agents for a face-to-face meeting

Before meeting with an agent, make sure they meet your minimum criteria, in addition to the referrals and online reviews you've already explored. Your criteria can vary, but here are my must-haves. Solid candidates should:

- Specialize in the geographical location in which you want to buy or sell
- Work as full-time, professional realtors
- Buy and sell a minimum of two properties per month, on average

To save time, you could simply call the agents on your shortlist, introduce yourself, and explain that you're having preliminary conversations with agents. Ask if they have 5-10 minutes for you and pose a handful of questions, such as:

- In which areas of the city do you specialize?
- Are you a full-time realtor?
- How long have you been in the profession?
- How many clients did you successfully help to buy or sell a home last year?

*DID YOU KNOW?

Many realtors don't work in the profession full time. According to the U.S. National Association of Realtors, the average agent closes about six deals per year, and about 10 per cent of licensed realtors conduct 90 per cent of all real estate activity. In order to maintain good industry relation-ships, understand the current market, and conduct effective negotiations, I believe an agent or team has to be active in your neighbourhood and do at least a couple transactions per month.

4. The personal interview

It's time to get to know the agents you've chosen. In the indus-try, we often refer to these meetings as "presentations." A listing presentation is for homeowners looking to sell, while a buyer's presentation is for potential buyers. Many consumers are moving up, or downsizing, so of course, these sessions can be combined. However, I don't love the term "presentation." To me, it implies one-way communication, with the agent doing most of the talking, when in fact, the most productive meetings are open, two-way con-versations between you and the agent.

A realtor will want to explain their process, the industry, and the market, but they should also want to get to know you. If they ask open-ended questions that don't lead you to their desired conclu-sions, they're sincerely learning what you need and considering how they can design a strategy to help you.

If you feel comfortable, you can openly share information about your preferred timeline, price range, wants and needs in a new home, details about your current home, and more – if these agents have already committed to extend the protections of an agency relationship. While you may interview more than one agent before making your choice, every B.C. agent you meet with will have disclosed in writing whether or not they're committing to the four legal duties, including the duty to keep your informa-tion confidential.

The candidates should be excited to talk about their business: where they work, who they work with, what they charge, what's covered in the fee, how they research market conditions, how they negotiate, and more. All of these topics are fair game.

My final listing presentation

About five years into my real estate career, before I hired my first team member, I received a call from a family with two young children who wanted to sell their current home and purchase a larger one. I had been recommended to them by a neighbour, and they wanted to meet with me to talk about representing them.

They told me that they were interviewing five realtors. Given the number of competitors for this listing, and my relative inexperience at the time, I figured I didn't have a chance. So, I decided not to compete, but simply to sit with this couple and answer their questions. I learned about their home, their timeline, their dreams for their new home, and tried to help them make the best decision they could for their family, without considering whether I might be their chosen professional.

I asked a lot of questions and listened intently to their answers. We explored ideas and strategies. I made suggestions about timing, preparation, and more, and I left their home feeling good about the meeting.

What do you think happened? Yep, I got the listing. I won against more experienced and successful agents by focusing the meeting on the clients, instead of on me.

From that moment on, I changed how I conduct initial meetings with both buyers and sellers. By shifting from presentation to dialogue, I learn enough to start building a strategy that will help them achieve their goals. I don't have the statistics to back this up, but I believe I land more listings and buyers because potential clients can tell I'm not trying to win.

Preparing for the interview

Formulating a list of questions will help you gain more information than if you simply plan to listen. It shows the agent you've done your research, and encourages authentic, two-way dialogue, which builds rapport and strengthens understanding.

You might ask:

1. When were you licensed?

2. Are you a full-time realtor?

3. Do you work as part of a team?

4. How many agents do you work with, and would you be my main contact?

5. Do you have an assistant for marketing and administration?

6. Do you have any professional designations, or have you taken additional training beyond the courses required for your licence?

7. What is your fee?

8. How do you market your listings?

9. Are there any marketing expenses that are not covered by your fee?

10. What areas of the city do you specialize in?

11. What are the current market conditions in my neighbour-hood, or the area I'm interested in?

12. Do you prefer competitive or collaborative negotia-tion tactics?

13. Do you offer a written summary of the property documents when I write an offer?

14. Do you have the capacity to take me on as a buyer and/or seller? How many clients can you serve at a given time?

You may not want or need to ask all of these questions, so choose the ones that interest you. Let your candidate take the lead and ask your questions along the way, or wait until the end to cover anything that wasn't addressed. Remember: there aren't necessarily any right or wrong answers to these questions. You're looking for the agent who's right for you.

Once you've had two or three of these meetings, you should know which of the agents possess the five attributes I outlined above, and one will likely stand out from the pack. This person will be qualified, confident, committed to service, and proud of what they're offering: the best possible experience and outcome.

5. Commit to your chosen agent and build your strategy

This can be a written commitment or a handshake, depending on the rules and norms in your particular market. The commitment you and your agent make to each other is the beginning of your partnership. Now you can begin to build your strategy, whether you're buying, selling, or both.

The relationship you have with your realtor is utterly unique. I can't think of another professional service like it. You're the boss, you're paying your realtor, and it's your home. The realtor works on your behalf and with your permission, often in writing and often verbally.

At the same time, your agent is the expert. They bring their knowledge, experience, relationships, and service to the table. You can trust them to help you make informed decisions. You'll probably meet with your agent several times per week and get to know them well during this time. It's extremely important to choose someone with the right set of skills, experience, and personal traits, so they can offer you the best experience and results.

When a close friend is a new realtor

What if a close friend or family member has just been licensed as a realtor – and you want them to represent you in your purchase or sale? Perhaps you want to hire them because you trust them explicitly, because you want to give them the business, or both.

I suggest you exercise caution here. New realtors do have some advantages: they've recently completed their coursework, so they often adhere closely to the industry's ethical guidelines. They can be highly motivated, hard-working, and genuinely client-focused, but they don't know what they don't know.

Educational requirements for B.C. real estate agents have become more stringent in recent years, but this is still a profession where much is learned on the job. Countless scenarios can emerge during a transaction; if your agent hasn't encountered enough variations yet, they may not be prepared to help you achieve the ideal outcome – despite their best intentions.

Consider asking your friend or family member to partner with a more experienced agent. If you're selling, this is called a co-list, which is not uncommon. If you're buying, this approach will take a little more coordination, but it's certainly possible. Your agent friend gets the benefit of a hands-on learning experience with a knowledgeable agent, and you get to work with someone you love and trust, while leveraging the skillset, relationships, and professional systems the stronger agent has developed over many years.

Selling a home in one location and buying in another

What if you're selling your family home in Coquitlam and buying in East Vancouver? If your agent is doing or has done exemplary work selling your home, you might want to extend that relationship for your purchase. But as we discussed earlier, it can be advantageous for buyers to work with agents who know their own local markets. There's no cut-and-dried answer to this question.

The trust and affection you have for your current realtor is no small thing, so I suggest you have an honest conversation about their experience and comfort level representing you in another market. Does your agent have experience in Vancouver? Do they know the properties and the people who work there? If not, would they consider partnering with another agent to give you the benefit of your trusting relationship, and the knowledge and expertise of a local specialist? Perhaps your agent has a colleague who specializes in the neighbourhood you want to buy in and would prefer to refer you to that agent, but would also want to stay in touch and help you along the way.

This chapter has provided a framework to help you choose your realtor. Don't worry if you don't yet feel confident evaluating candidates' skill sets. As you learn more about listing and buying strategies, how market statistics and macroeconomic factors weigh into your decision-making, and we explore a little negotiation theory, you'll feel better prepared to choose a talented and client-focused team in your area.

Listing strategies: preparation and timing

Acouple of years after I bought that perfect, spacious, two-bedroom condo, my financial advisor made a suggestion. He noted that in just two years, my home had increased in value by about 25 per cent; an astonishing return. He proposed that I sell the condo and allow him to invest the proceeds on my behalf. He said it would be better to diversify my portfolio rather than holding all that equity in one investment (my home).

According to his calculations, I'd have over $100,000 to work with – a chunk of cash I'd never had before. I have to admit, the advisor's idea appealed to me. But first, I called my realtor to ask for his opinion. I filled him in, and then he asked two questions:

"How are you enjoying your home?"

Short answer? I loved it. The condo was affordable and extremely comfortable for the three of us. We lived within walking distance of everything we needed. We'd done some renovations and were happy with how they turned out.

"Where would you live if you sold your home?"

I admitted that I hadn't worked that out, but we'd probably rent an apartment in the same area.

After I answered those questions, my realtor, Dale, said he didn't think I should sell it. In fact, I remember his exact words: "Real estate will stand you in good stead, Mary."

When I think back to that conversation, I'm so grateful for his perspective. His advice went against his own interest. After all, he would have had the property listing and sales fee. But if I had sold the condo and rented my home, I would have missed the next four years of appreciation – and I may never have been able to buy back into the Vancouver market.

Buying and selling at the same time is the best way to protect yourself from market fluctuations. Whenever a client says they want to sell a property, rent, and then buy back in when the market craters, I ask what they'll do if the market doesn't cooperate with their plans.

This story reflects my own experiences and perspectives. You might feel differently. There are many different choices that you and your realtor will make together – and finding the right time to sell your home is just one of the topics we'll cover in the following chapters.

Listing a home is never a one-size-fits-all proposition. Your property characteristics, preferences, market conditions, and other factors will all come into play. Knowing some of the considerations and decisions we make when designing a marketing strategy will empower you to participate more fully in the process.

We'll also break down the listing agreement that you and your agent will sign before your home hits the market.

CHAPTER 4:
LISTING PREPARATION AND TIMING

*I*n real estate, like many things in life, you often enjoy better results when you plan ahead. Let's touch on some details to consider in the weeks, or even months, before you put your home on the market, such as:

- Is there a time of year, or a season, when your home will show better to prospective buyers?

- Do you have small children or pets? Could you time your listing to coincide with a vacation to make showings and open houses easier for your family?

- Do you have a tenant in your investment property or basement suite? What steps can you take to ensure a smooth process for them – and for yourself?

- What smart renovations or maintenance projects could add value to your property?

Your realtor will guide you through the preparation process and offer insights to optimize the sale price and improve the experience.

With thoughtful planning, you can boost your property value with some low-cost decorative changes, small fixes, or even a complete renovation. You could time your listing to coincide with favourable weather conditions, more hours of sunlight, or to minimize inconvenience to your family and/or tenants. All of these considerations have the potential to make the entire process easier for you, to put more money in your pocket – or both.

Many sellers can do the cleaning and decluttering required to ensure their home sparkles, both online and during viewings and open houses, a week or two before listing day. However, some things take more time, so it's important to plan ahead.

Timing

"What's the best time of year to sell – especially if I want to get the highest price for my home?"

I hear this question a lot, and the answer is, **it varies.**

Spring typically attracts the most buyers. As the days get warmer, drier, and longer, buyers begin to engage. But, this doesn't mean you'll get a higher sale price, because there are also typically more sellers, or more competition for your home.

"Should I sell now, or will my home sell for more if I wait until next year?"

Sadly, your agent can't accurately answer this question. I wish I could! There have been countless times when economists and/or realtors predicted a significant market change – and it didn't happen. Economists, for example, didn't foresee the 2008 U.S. subprime mortgage crisis, the Covid-19 pandemic, or the rapid rise in interest rates and inflation that followed the pandemic.

A skilled agent can tell you what has happened in your local market, what usually happens, what's happening right now, and how prices are trending, but none of us can see the future. Realtors sometimes make predictions, and that's okay. If you and your agent talk about future market conditions, just know that these are opinions and not facts. Don't make critical decisions based solely on an opinion – even an educated one.

We all wish we could time the market to buy low and sell high, but unfortunately, that just isn't realistic. Most people choose to buy and sell at the same time to protect themselves from market fluctuations they can't control or predict.

So, if spring isn't always the best time, and you can't predict future market conditions, here are some other factors that can affect your timing.

Seasonal considerations

Elements including light, weather, heat, the school calendar, and other factors can all affect how potential buyers see your home. As you consider what makes your home unique, the goal is to maximize the positive features and minimize the potential challenges. Here are some examples:

- Air conditioning isn't common in Vancouver (and many other B.C. municipalities). If your home has this feature, consider selling in the summer or early fall. The homes you'll compete with will be seasonally warm. By comparison, yours will be cool and comfortable, which will stand out on a blistering day. This also applies to ground floor condo suites. Potential buyers will appreciate a cooler unit on an airless summer day.

- If selling an air conditioned home when it's hot is smart, it follows that a southwest-facing corner condo on the 12th floor – with floor-to-ceiling windows that open just a crack – will show better in cool weather. Buyers will love all the winter light, and they won't feel the summer heat during viewings.

- Does your home face a busy street? Wet pavement amplifies road noise, so consider selling in late spring through to fall. You'll have a better chance of dry roads.

- Does your home have a beautiful garden or patio? Consider selling in the late spring when you can maximize your home's curb appeal and stage that outdoor living space.

Your next move could also affect the ideal timing. For example, are you buying another home in the same neighbourhood? If so, consider when you'll have more properties to choose from when shopping for your new home. Inventory tends to build in the spring, drop during the summer, rise again in the fall, and hit a low point in December and early January.

Whether to buy first, or sell first, is another critical decision if you're buying and selling in the same market. Most home sellers will also be buying a new home, and will need the money from that sale to make their purchase. This presents one of the most difficult decisions you'll make; whether to buy first, or sell first. There are risks and benefits associated with both approaches.

If you buy first and the market shifts before you sell your home, or the market doesn't respond as favourably as you expected, you may have to accept a lower-than-expected price to avoid being stuck with two homes and two mortgages.

If you sell first, you may not be able to quickly find your next home – and prices could rise in the meantime. You could also get priced out of the type of home you want, or have to settle for one you don't love, just so you have somewhere to live.

Knowing the worst-case scenarios can help you make a decision that's right for you. And with research and careful planning, you can mitigate the risks. It may seem unresolvable, but people buy and sell homes every day. They make it work – and so can you.

Should I buy or sell first? What to consider

First, maybe you don't need to make this decision at all. You could include a subject to sale clause in your offer to buy a home.

The subject to sale clause allows you to secure a property and then list your home. If your home doesn't sell in the time frame agreed to in the contract, you're released from your obligation to buy the new property. This approach can work well in some markets, but it's next to impossible in others.

Increasingly, many real estate markets have structurally low inventory – meaning there are rarely enough homes to satisfy demand. Greater Vancouver, for example, is almost always characterized as a seller's market. Vancouver is surrounded by mountains, ocean, and farmland with decades of single-family zoning in most of the land allocated to housing. We rarely have an abundance of supply compared to demand. In a strong seller's market, homeowners are unlikely to accept an offer that includes a subject to sale clause. They simply don't have to.

Even when a seller does accept a subject to sale, they'll almost always insist on a time clause. There are variations, but generally speaking, the time clause states that upon acceptance of another offer, a seller can give the buyer 24-72 hours to remove the subject to sale clause. This usually isn't enough time to get a firm offer on the buyer's sale, so you're left with the same decision: take the risk or lose the property.

Finally, if a seller accepts an offer with a subject to sale clause, it might indicate that the property is priced above market value. The seller is happy to work with your offer because no one else is willing to pay their price. Do you want to pay more to avoid risk? You might be better off listing your current home and hoping the property you want is still on the market once you've sold. At that point, you can write a stronger offer and retain more negotiating power.

If you're determined to avoid risk, it's good to know that the subject to sale clause exists – even if it's an imperfect solution. Now we'll weigh the pros and cons of listing first and buying first, because in all likelihood, if you're planning to buy and sell in the same market, you'll choose one of these two options.

Listing first

In this scenario, you list your home for sale and secure an offer before submitting an offer on another home.

Pros:

- You know exactly what your home sold for, which clarifies what you can afford to buy (assuming you need that equity, as most of us do to make our next move)

- You know which dates to include in your offer to purchase another property, because you know when you have to move out of your current home

- There's no risk of buying a home and finding that your current home doesn't sell in time to use the equity to complete your purchase – resulting in high borrowing costs if you have to carry both mortgages at once, or a legal battle as you try to revoke a firm deal on the buying side

Cons:

- You've sold your current home, which means the clock is ticking on your search for a new home

- If you don't find one during that time, you may have to get a short-term rental, which could increase costs and require you to move twice

- If inventory is low and demand is high, it may take several weeks to secure your new home. In a rising market, home prices can increase month over month. This reduces your affordability, because you sold when prices were lower than when you finally buy back in

How to mitigate the risks of selling first

- Take at least one exploratory tour with your realtor before you list your home. See what's currently on the market in your price range. Knowing the available options can make you feel more comfortable selling your home before you've bought a new one.

- When you're negotiating an offer on your current home, push for the longest possible closing and possession dates so you have ample time to shop for your new home. In a strong seller's market, you may be able to build in some flexibility – giving you the ability to adjust the dates with your buyer once you find your new home.

- Ensure buying is your top priority after you've sold. Put your agent on speed dial, keep an open mind, and view as many homes as possible. Take the time you need to make a good choice, but try not to let too much time pass between selling and buying.

Buying first

In this scenario, you'll start by shopping for your new home. Once you have a purchase contract in place, you'll immediately list your home.

Pros:

- You likely won't have to vacate your current home before it's time to move into your new one

- You can take your time in the buying cycle and find the right fit – without any deadline pressure

Cons:

- You don't know the exact sale price of your current home, so you won't know precisely what you can afford when you choose your new home

- The purchase contract will lock in your moving date. That means you probably can't match the dates a prospective buyer for your home may want

- If you need the equity from your current home, you'll have a deadline to sell your property. If your current property doesn't sell before you have to pay for the home you bought, you may be stuck carrying two mortgages at once – meaning you'll pay extra interest and you could take a big financial hit

- You may feel pressured to accept a lower sale price on your home in order to sell it before you have to pay for your new home

How to mitigate the risks of buying first

- While searching for your new home, prepare your current home for sale by decluttering, repainting, doing any necessary landscaping work, etc

- List your home immediately after you have an accepted purchase offer

- Price your home to attract attention. List it near the lower end of your estimated market value range, and perhaps even a bit lower. You don't have the luxury of trying a high price to see what happens. If you're locked into a purchase contract and you have to sell, you need to get the list price right the first time in order to attract a buyer.

For most people, selling before buying is the best approach – simply to dodge the worst-case scenario of owning two homes at once. The financial consequences of carrying both mortgages can be more severe than paying for a short-term rental, which is the worst-case scenario if you choose to sell first.

That said, there are myriad factors that influence this decision and, as usual, one size rarely fits all. Talk to your realtor and lender about your property, the market, and your own financial situation to determine which approach carries the least risk and offers the most benefit for you. Once you make a decision, you and your agent will execute your strategy to mitigate the risks you can't avoid completely.

Family/tenant coordination:

It's important to consider what works best for your family and your tenants, if you have them, when preparing your home for sale.

- Homes typically show better, sell faster, and achieve a higher price when they're clean and staged. This condition is easier to maintain when kids, pets, and tenants are not at home. If it's possible to list while you're on vacation, your agent will know that the home is always exactly as they left it and they have around-the-clock access for viewings.

- Listing when your tenants are away is especially beneficial, because they may resent the intrusion and inconvenience of frequent showings. After all, tenants have nothing to gain and everything to lose if someone buys the home they're renting.

*DID YOU KNOW?

Tenants have entrenched rights that can complicate the selling process for homeowners. For example, tenants require ample notice before showings, they have the right to stay in their home for viewings, and they can ask not to have their space photographed. A potential buyer who plans to evict your tenant also presents challenges that are (rightly) tricky to navigate.

If you're selling a tenanted property, plan ahead and involve your realtor early in the process. The B.C. Residential Tenancy Branch doesn't allow landlords to evict tenants in order to sell a home, so it's important to consider how you can encourage their cooperation.

Preparing to sell your home

The condition of your home can make it more valuable to a potential buyer, or even entice multiple buyers to make an offer. Many of the steps you'll take to boost your home's appeal can be done in the week leading up to the listing. You can work with your agent on those details. Some, however, take more time, so consider these options well before you want to go to market.

Limited renovations

Some high-impact, low-cost renovations could help you secure a higher sales price. Short of a full-scale renovation, you probably have some deferred maintenance tasks that are well worth your time, such as repairing a fence, weeding or trimming the garden, tightening door handles, swapping light fixtures, or adding a fresh coat of interior or exterior paint. These can be done in the weeks before you list your home.

Full-scale renovations

Some home sellers choose to undertake larger renovations to add value before selling. For example, a new kitchen, updated bathrooms, and fresh flooring will almost always increase the sale price. This approach works well if a home is vacant and construction can be done quickly with minimal disruptions. It's especially advantageous when a homeowner has enough expertise to do the work themselves. If you're living in the property and need to hire a contractor to renovate, this becomes a less attractive option, for several reasons:

- Renovations are expensive
- Obtaining permits, strata permission (if applicable), finding the right tradespeople, and securing time in their schedule, can be complicated and time-consuming
- It's much easier for a buyer to replace the flooring, for example, when the home is vacant than when you're still living there

If you decide to hire a painter, handyman, or contractor, shop around for competitive quotes. Your agent should be able to share trusted contacts, whether you choose a small or a substantial renovation.

Decluttering

Almost all of us have too much stuff, which is abundantly clear when it's time to list our homes. Spend a few minutes browsing online listings and you'll see that most homes look clean and spacious because the seller has stashed away daily necessities (blender, toothbrushes, coffee maker, big comfy chair, and family photos). Much of this can be done in the last few days, but if you collect antique clocks, for example, or you have extremely large furniture, consider selling or storing some items. This will also give your realtor room to work their staging magic.

Meet with your realtor early in the process to make key decisions about renovations, small fixes, decluttering, and timing. Depending how much work your home needs, and whether you're accommodating tenants, your preparation time could vary from a few weeks to several months before listing day.

The listing agreement

To list your property on REALTOR.ca and other real estate websites, you and your agent must agree to a number of terms and conditions using a listing agreement.

This is rarely the most riveting part of the process, but it's important to:

- Discuss the critical role of the listing agreement in the home-selling process
- Understand the legally binding nature of the real estate listing contract
- Become familiar with the terms and conditions within the listing agreement

The listing agreement is a standard industry contract that outlines the terms and conditions agreed to by a home seller and their realtor, and the responsibilities of both parties. These include the real estate fee and percentage shared with the buyer's brokerage, the list price of the home, the dates the listing is in effect, and more.

The agreement is a lengthy, lawyer-drafted document designed to protect both you and your agent. Most of it can't be changed without additional legal advice.

This contract is legally binding. Once both parties have signed it, neither can unilaterally decide to cancel or change it. Since your agent knows this form inside and out, and has used it hundreds of times, it's in your best interest to become familiar with it, too.

Your agent is required to explain this document in detail with you before you sign on the dotted line. The agreement is several pages long, so ideally, your realtor will give you time to read it over and highlight any questions before you meet for signing. The better you understand this document, the more time and energy you can spend on your listing strategy.

It's convenient (and tempting) for both realtors and home sellers to sign documents digitally, but I strongly recommend that you discuss the listing contract in person. Signing is an opportunity to discuss what's in this critical document and how the listing process will unfold. It's also an opportunity to strengthen trust and understanding between you and your realtor.

You'll find a current example of the BCREA Multiple Listing Contract in the Resource Guide, as well as a document explaining each term. If you're keen to have a better understanding of this important contract, have a look.

Real estate marketing: the four Ps in the marketing mix

CHAPTER 5:
MARKETING

There's one concept I learned in university that I've applied to every job I've held since, and I still use every day in my real estate career. That's the Marketing Mix, or the Four Ps:

- Product

- Price

- Promotion

- Place

It seemed obvious to me that "product" was the most important element of the marketing plan. Successful companies don't design, build, develop, or buy a product and then determine how to market it; they first consider what their consumer wants and then design, build, develop, or buy that product. When a product satisfies a consumer's needs or wants, the other elements in the marketing mix can achieve truly exceptional results. Even the sharpest advertising and promotion is pointless without a great product.

In real estate, most of the work your realtor does to market your home is designed to add value to your product, making it more desirable to the consumer. If this doesn't make sense right now, don't worry, it will.

In this section, you'll learn some practical steps that you and your realtor can take to improve your product. You'll learn what you can expect from your agent and how you can help to maximize exposure for your home, in any market conditions. We'll focus on product, place, and promotion. Pricing strategy is a big topic, so we'll cover that in the next section.

With some basic marketing knowledge, you and your realtor can ensure your home is best positioned to compete with other listings and to attract at least one, and potentially multiple offers. Knowing why your agent is making suggestions that will, in some cases, cost you time and money, will empower you to accept or reject those suggestions and feel confident about your decisions.

Marketing versus selling

Simply put, marketing is about exposure. It's a one-sided communication that broadcasts information such as features, photographs, and location to potential customers online, in the media, or through signage or printed materials. Selling is a skill set your agent uses alongside marketing efforts when dealing directly with potential buyers and their agents. Personal selling is a two-way communication, whereby your agent listens and offers up the features and benefits of a home, and provides other details to encourage or negotiate an offer.

Real estate marketing is a multifaceted way to promote properties in order to attract local or international buyers.

Four pillars of the marketing plan

Product – What are you selling?

Price – What is the published or listing price?

Promotion – Paid advertising, point-of-sale signage, flyers, brochures, etc.

Place – Where can people find the product or service?*

*Place has a different meaning in real estate than when marketing a product like toothpaste. Your home physically occupies one place. It sits on one street, in one city, whereas you can find toothpaste for sale in Costco, Safeway, Amazon, Walmart, and many other places. In the real estate context, place is where people can find the listing online, usually on websites such as REALTOR.ca, agents' websites, Facebook, Instagram, real estate publications such as REW.ca, and more.

Product

Marketing 101 teaches us that the most effective businesses consider their product as part of the marketing mix, not separate from it. In a practical sense, this means designing offerings – whether they're goods, services, or consulting – to meet the wants and needs of a given consumer. Smart businesses know their audience before they create their product. And the product includes packaging. Apple products are perhaps the best example, because the company's sleek, clean packaging is integral to the experience of buying an iPhone, AirPods, or a laptop.

MYTH

In real estate, you as the seller have just one product: your home. Your product is that home, and it is what it is. There's no packaging, so we move on to price, right?

Wrong. As we discussed in Chapter 4, there are many things you and your realtor can do to make your product and packaging more valuable, which should elicit a higher sale price.

Preparing your home, or packaging your product, is the first piece of the marketing puzzle. Think of real estate packaging as the steps that prepare a home for listing, such as professional cleaning, maintenance, or smart renovations.

A deep cleaning and fixing small things like chipped paint, loose door handles, and mismatched lightbulbs shows buyers your home is well cared for. Next up are:

- Decluttering
- Staging or styling
- Curb appeal enhancements, such as gardening

Staging a home for photographs, both inside and out, ensures that the all-important first impression is a good one. When visitors come to experience your home in person, buyers can envision their life in a more open, comfortable, neutral space than our homes usually present from day to day.

These photographs were taken just four hours apart. The first was taken before staging and decluttering, and the second was taken when we were done. Which photo might encourage more buyers to call their agents to book a showing? Which might encourage a potential buyer to make an offer?

Before
Photo: Danielle Desjarlais

After.

Photo: B.C. Floor Plans

If you're living in the space, always try to return your home to showing condition for viewings and open houses.

The next step includes:

- Professional measurements / floor plans
- Documents such as city permits, oil tank scans, legal opinions on title searches, strata plans and documents, renovation receipts, and more

Providing documentation substantiates the value proposition, or the story we're telling in the marketing. For example, "this home has a great layout for families. It was substantially renovated with city permits by licensed contractors, and therefore, is worth more money than other homes that recently sold in the neighbourhood."

*DID YOU KNOW?

In a busy seller's market, buyers usually spend less than 30 minutes in a home before they make an offer. We often spend more time buying a car, a vacation, or even a pair of jeans. It's fascinating to consider how little time you have to grab your buyer's attention, given the size of the investment.

The time and money that you and your realtor spend to show a home at its best, both online and during that 30-minute viewing, is worthwhile to ensure you make an excellent first impression. Decluttering, staging, and detailed property information makes your home more desirable and, therefore, a more valuable product.

Place/Promotion

Traditionally, place and promotion are two different pillars of the marketing mix. Place is the channel where customers find a product or service, while promotion is advertising, publicity, or point-of-sale merchandising.

When marketing real estate, we put them together, because "place" isn't a physical location like a store; it's all the online places where a buyer can learn about your home, rather than the actual home. Many of the methods we use to promote homes live online as well, so place and promotion are a logical pairing.

MYTH

In a seller's market, I don't need to promote my home. It's in a great location. As long as it's listed on REALTOR.ca, it will sell for a great price.

A seller's market has more demand than supply. Vancouver, for example, is a structurally constrained market that typically favours sellers. We simply can't sprawl outward like many other cities. But that doesn't mean your home will sell for top dollar simply by uploading it to REALTOR.ca. Experienced realtors know that smart promotion ensures their listings have the best possible opportunity not only to sell, but also to sell for the highest price in any given market.

Promotion

Promotion includes all elements of the marketing plan that expose your home to as many buyers as possible. Your realtor will apply five key promotional tools:

- Online promotion
- Traditional or physical promotion
- Open houses / viewing appointments
- Neighbourhood engagement
- Signage

Online promotion

Virtually all home searches begin online. All the steps involved in promoting your home online are designed to encourage potential buyers to make an in-person visit. In some cases – such as working with an out-of-province buyer – the online presentation may be the only version of the product your buyers see before making an offer. With technology such as video, 3D floor plans, and virtual tours, a small percentage of buyers purchase a home without even stepping through the door.

Online promotion includes:

- Professional photographs
- Professional video tour
- Professional measurements and floor plan
- Social media posts and advertising
- Exposure on REALTOR.ca

- Exposure on your agent's website and other agents' sites
- Paid advertising on consumer sites like REW.ca
- Your agent's e-newsletter to clients and the real estate industry

Your agent can dramatically boost awareness of your home by including more than just the online listing in their marketing materials. Professionally measured floor plans and quality photos and video on real estate websites and social media give consumers more information in multiple formats. Some buyers love a video tour, while others don't have the patience to watch them. Some buyers actively search REALTOR.ca every day. Others are less engaged, but may find your listing on Instagram or Facebook and be intrigued enough to attend an open house.

Your agent's job is to not rely on a single channel, but to generate more exposure for your home.

Traditional or physical promotion

Most homes are now promoted extensively online. However, there's still room for proven, real-world tactics. Marketing materials that potential buyers can hold in their hands, early access for neighbours, and effective signage to catch people's eyes as they're walking by can complement our online efforts.

Quality full-colour brochures

Since buyers spend so little time in the homes they visit, it's important to offer them a high-quality brochure with several photographs, the professionally measured floor plan, and a list of the home's best features. This takeaway material helps them to remember your home, especially if they've seen several other homes in a short period of time.

A few years before I got into real estate, my husband and I were looking to move from our condo into a townhome, duplex, or even a small house. We weren't in a big rush, but we had a baby daughter and hoped to welcome a second child in the next couple years. We knew we'd need more space. So, we moved into research mode and started looking at a few properties each weekend; some with our agent, and some on our own.

After several weeks and many showings, we made an offer on a duplex, but we couldn't come together with the seller on price. Then we offered on a house and were blown out of the water in a bidding war. We were starting to feel discouraged.

One day, I was organizing a bookshelf and discovered the glossy brochure for a townhome in Vancouver's Mount Pleasant neighbourhood. We had viewed it three weeks earlier when we were still hoping we could afford a house. So, while I remembered liking it, we hadn't pursued an offer at that time. As I flipped through the pages, I saw my handwritten note that read "Perfect!" I showed it to my husband that night and we wrote an offer the next day. We bought that home and lived there happily for nine years with our two daughters. If I hadn't found the brochure when I did, I doubt we would have circled back to the townhome. That was a powerful piece of paper.

Great photographs, videos, and online promotions can entice potential buyers to call their realtor and visit your home, but don't forget the power of promotional materials such as print brochures and flyers.

Neighbourhood open houses or sneak peeks

Who knows your neighbourhood better than the people who live within a few blocks of you? Extending special invitations to your neighbours and letting them know you've listed your home can be a great way to spread the word. Highlight your home's special features and indicate when they can come to view it. Creating an invite-only viewing party with refreshments can also make guests feel special and encourage them to tell their friends about your home.

Signage

Placing signs on the lawn or in front of the building encourages people to look it up online. Sometimes house hunters – especially local buyers – love a certain building, street, or even your house. Potential buyers often call listing realtors because they saw the sign out front.

CHAPTER 6:
SHOWING YOUR HOME TO POTENTIAL BUYERS

Most real estate transactions happen because a motivated buyer makes an appointment to view a home with their realtor. They like the home, write an offer, and buy the home. Most qualified, motivated buyers work with an agent, and they'll see the home while touring properties with their realtor. These appointments are managed differently depending on the situation and the preferences of the homeowner, realtor, or team.

Store keys in a lockbox

In this scenario, your realtor leaves a set of keys in a secure lockbox somewhere on your property. The best option is a lockbox sanctioned by the real estate boards. These work with a cellphone app that ensures only realtors have access, and the code changes with every showing. The buyer's agent makes an appointment, accesses the lockbox to retrieve the keys, shows the property, and returns the keys afterward. The application notifies the listing agent that the lockbox has opened and been closed up again.

Some agents use what's known as a carpenter's lockbox. I don't recommend these, because the code doesn't change. Anyone who has the code can access it. If your agent uses lockboxes, insist they use the most secure type. This approach ensures your listing agent never has to refuse a showing request if they're unavailable; the buyer's agent can accompany their client and unlock the door. Lockboxes are especially convenient for solo agents and agents who cover larger geographical areas. They aren't widely used in the City of Vancouver, perhaps because everything is a relatively short distance away.

Unlicensed assistant provides access

Some real estate teams have unlicensed assistants who can provide access to their listings (your home). When a team member isn't licensed, it simply means they aren't a realtor. They perform functions such as marketing, administration, errands, staging, and support other essential parts of the business. You may prefer to have an unlicensed assistant open your home rather than letting buyer's agents visit alone with their clients, for two key reasons:

- The team member can arrive early to turn on the lights, open windows or blinds, fluff the pillows, and do a last-minute tidy to ensure the home is ready for viewing.

- You, as the homeowner, may feel more comfortable knowing a member of the team you hired is the only one who holds your keys and can close the blinds, ensure your pets remain safely inside (if applicable), and lock up properly.

It's important to note that an unlicensed team member can't show your home to a buyer without the buyer's realtor present. There are also limits to the information this team member can provide about your home. They can answer factual questions, assuming they have a list provided by the agent, such as the age of the roof. They can't, however, answer qualitative questions, which could help to explain the features and benefits of your home.

Your agent or another agent on the team shows your home

Lastly, your agent or another agent on the team (sometimes referred to as a showing specialist) can personally show your home. This is by far the most effective and secure approach. After all, there's an art to successfully showing a home; having your agent present at every showing gives you a major advantage.

Your agent knows that every viewing appointment could introduce your home to a buyer who falls in love and makes an offer. Your agent will arrive early to turn on the lights, maybe play some soft music, or turn on the fireplace. On a sunny day, they'll open the patio doors and windows and set up the outdoor furniture.

An experienced agent will warmly greet the buyer and their agent, and invite them to take their time in the space. Your agent can also tell visitors what else they need to know, such as the presence of a cat or a tenant in the home. Your agent will start by doing more listening than talking, because:

1. They want the buyer to experience the home in a low-pressure environment. A calm, relaxed vibe encourages buyers to explore what interests them most, imagine themselves living there, and consider whether this home could work for them – without an annoying or distracting sales pitch.

2. They want the buyer's agent to share your home's best features with their buyer. This is important, because the buyer's agent knows their client. They know what's important to them, and what they've seen and either rejected or lost out on, so they're in a better position than your agent to highlight details their client truly cares about.

Your agent's next steps depend on what they see in those first few minutes:

- What is the relationship like between the buyer and their agent?

- Have they seen a lot of homes together, or is today the first day?

- Is the buyer's agent prepared with information about your home?

- Does the buyer's agent know the local schools and neighbourhood amenities?

In the best-case scenario, the buyer's agent knows their client well, has studied the property details, and knows the neighbourhood. They're comfortable talking about your home, and may ask a clarifying question of your agent, but for the most part, they guide their client through your home and have a two-way conversation.

Your agent will accompany them as they tour the home; giving them space, but staying nearby to answer questions and chime in when appropriate. A great showing specialist is like a server in a Michelin-starred restaurant; always there when you need them, but never hovering.

On occasion, a buyer's agent isn't prepared or doesn't have the knowledge and experience to maximize the experience for their buyer. In those instances, it's your agent's job to communicate the best parts of your home and neighbourhood to the buyer and the agent.

Another benefit of this arrangement is that your agent has an opportunity to learn something about the buyer or their agent, and build rapport with both of them. If they do end up writing an offer, this connection and information can give you and your agent an edge in the negotiation.

Open houses

I love open houses because they make life easier for my sellers, particularly during the first week their home is listed. Rather than juggling individual appointments at different times throughout that week, many agents will opt to come through the open house with their clients, or even send the buyer through on their own. It's especially helpful for families, and sellers with pets or tenants, to be able to plan for two or three open houses during the first week, rather than countless separate appointments.

Open houses are often scheduled on Saturdays and Sundays from 2-4pm, but this varies. Sometimes an agent will choose a different time if it's advantageous, such as a Saturday morning if the eastern light is stunning – or if they choose to serve mimosas and muffins.

Open houses increase the number of people who will view your home in person – and that's usually a good thing.

*DID YOU KNOW?

There are instances when it's better not to host an open house, such as during a buyer's market (when supply is greater than demand). Some U.S. and Canadian markets experienced this scenario during the last half of 2023 when interest rates rose quickly in both countries. The high rates created uncertainty and reduced affordability, and therefore, lowered demand. Your agent may advise you not to have an open house so qualified buyers don't see how few other buyers are interested.

If your home faces a busy street, they may also want to skip the open house. In this case, your agent may want to show your home individually so they can create the best conditions for the buyer, with closed windows and soft music playing, for example. At an open house, a buyer who wasn't previously concerned about traffic noise may hear other visitors discussing the sound and turn them off the location. That buyer may decide not to offer, or may offer less, because of comments others make while touring the space.

The right marking strategies are different in every situation. You and your agent will work together to decide how to best show your home. For example, will you use a combination of one-on-one appointments with qualified buyers and open houses for everyone, or choose one or the other? If you do opt for viewing appointments, will your keys be in a secure lockbox on the property for buyer's agents to access, or will your agent personally show your home? In any case, your agent will give you as much notice as possible so you can return your home to showing condition.

Security tip:

Regardless of whether you choose private showings, open houses, or a combination, it's smart to remove or lock up valuables, particularly small items. It's rare for things to go missing during open houses and appointments, but it's prudent to store jewellery, small electronics, and other precious items out of sight.

Your home deserves a custom marketing strategy

We've covered some of the most common promotional tools, but your imagination is the only limit. Community centre or coffee shop bulletin boards, colourful flyers, online postings, and real estate features in print media are all avenues realtors can use to get more exposure for their listings.

Marketing real estate is a creative exercise. Your agent will design a custom strategy to present your home in its best light, price it to attract the right buyers, and expose it to as many buyers as possible through advertising, social media, professional marketing materials, personal invitations, and other tools.

Be curious, ask questions, give feedback, and share your own ideas, if you like. As I've said, you and your realtor are partners, so don't be afraid to express your preferences. Agents do better work when they explain the process along the way. It holds us accountable, helps us think outside the box, and ensures we can customize parts of the plan just for you.

Fair market value and pricing strategy

There's a common industry misconception that home sellers set home prices. The reality is that while home sellers set their list price, the sale price is decided by both the buyer and the seller. It's the buyer who writes an offer, or accepts a counter offer and ultimately agrees to pay a certain price; a price the seller is willing to accept. In other words, it takes two to tango.

Usually, home values are based on a combination of factors: the home's unique qualities, the yard and lot size (if it's a house), the desirability of the location, and more. Sometimes, the market value isn't in the house at all, but in the land – such as when a neighbourhood has been rezoned for higher-density construction. In this example, the home's current condition is irrelevant, because the buyer is purchasing the land to build a duplex, townhome complex, or condo building. For rural properties, land may be more valuable when it has natural resources such as oil, minerals, or timber.

When realtors represent home sellers, we help them to choose the list price most likely to attract a buyer, or ideally more than one buyer, so we can negotiate the best possible sale price.

To explain how we arrive at these recommendations, let's explore:

• Fair market value

- Comparative market analysis
- Buyer's, seller's, and balanced markets

Once we've covered these concepts, we'll discuss how they inform pricing strategies. We'll outline three pricing approaches and weigh the pros and cons of each.

CHAPTER 7:
WHAT IS FAIR MARKET VALUE?

*I*n real estate, fair market value is the price a buyer is willing to pay and a seller is willing to accept in an arm's length transaction – assuming the property has been appropriately exposed to the marketplace. An arm's length transaction means the buyer and seller were unknown to each other, and there's no reason why the seller might have sold the home for less than it was worth, such as to a grown child, or a good friend.

Since each property is different, the market is always changing, and each buyer and seller have their own means and motivations, we don't know a property's fair market value until after it sells. Your agent can't tell you when you sign the listing agreement exactly what that number will turn out to be.

Understanding fair market value is fundamental to buying and selling real estate. Without it, we couldn't give our buyers context around an offer price. We couldn't advise our sellers on a listing price. In many ways, we measure our success in a negotiation by whether we've achieved or exceeded our clients' expectations in relation to this value.

Fair market value: a case study

Mr. Smith wants to sell his Main Street townhome and lists it with a boutique real estate firm. His agent presents a thorough comparative market analysis that suggests the property's fair market value sits between $1.45 million and $1.525 million. Together, they decide to list the home for $1.5 million on a Monday morning.

The agent effectively markets the home: staging, designing beautiful brochures, hiring a professional photographer and videographer, and engaging a measurement technician who produces an accurate floor plan. The agent buys Facebook ads, shares the listing on Instagram, holds an agent's tour preview, and two weekend open houses.

The agent also books private showings for realtors during the week. They'll accept offers on the following Tuesday – eight days after the home is listed. The buyer, Mrs. Anderson, doesn't know Mr. Smith, and views the home with her agent on the weekend. She loves it and writes an offer for $1.4 million on Tuesday. Luckily for her, there are no other offers. After some negotiation, Mr. Smith accepts Mrs. Anderson's final counter offer of $1.485 million.

Case study questions

Q - Why does it matter whether the listing agent effectively marketed the property?

A - The definition of fair market value requires that the sale price is achieved after a property is appropriately exposed to the market. This means potential buyers have a reasonable chance to, most likely, see the listing online and book a showing or attend an open house. To ensure this, an agent has to list the home's features and benefits correctly, create reasonably effective marketing materials, and actively promote the listing by emailing it to other agents in their office, for example. An agent should also share and advertise it on social media, and upload it to websites such as REALTOR.ca, Real Estate Weekly, and others.

Q - Why does it matter that the agent hosted several showings, an agent's preview, and two open houses before reviewing offers?

A - If the listing agent had effectively marketed and advertised the property, but accepted an offer after just one showing, they wouldn't know if other buyers were willing to offer on the home. Could a bidding war have driven up the sale price? By holding offers for a week, allowing private appointments, hosting an agent's preview and two open houses prior to reviewing offers, both the agent and Mr. Smith knew that if only one offer materialized on Tuesday, there were likely no other qualified buyers ready, willing, and able to write an offer on the home at that time.

Q - What is an arm's length transaction?

A - An arm's length transaction means there were no special circumstances that could affect the price, such as a husband selling to his ex-wife, or a deal between friends. In an arm's length transaction, the buyer and seller are unknown to each other. If they are acquainted, it's not a close enough relationship that the buyer might receive a price break, for example.

Usually the buyer and seller are represented by separate real estate professionals, each negotiating on their client's behalf. If Mr. Smith had sold his home privately to a neighbour, data would show what it sold for, but the price would have no relation to fair market value. Realtors wouldn't use that price when estimating the value of another, similar property in the neighbourhood.

Q - How does fair market value relate to list price?

A - The list price is rarely the final sale price, or fair market value. Sellers and their agents set the list price based on a combination of the seller's wishes, the agent's advice about market conditions, and the comparative market analysis, which we'll cover in the next chapter. The combination of the seller, the successful buyer, both realtors involved, and broadly, other prospective buyers, determines fair market value – which we only know once the property has sold. In this case study, the list price was a little higher than the final sale price, but this isn't always the case.

Q - Did Mr. Smith, with the help of his agent, achieve fair market value?

A - Yes – based on the information provided. The case study indicates that the home was properly exposed to the market through advertising, professional marketing materials, and buyers had many opportunities to view the home before the offer date. When an offer emerged, the listing agent negotiated with the buyer's agent, and the two parties reached an agreement. The buyer was willing to pay a figure the seller was willing to accept. The parties were unknown to each other and each represented by their own real estate agent.

*DID YOU KNOW?

Fair market value has no relationship to B.C. Assessment value. The province assesses property values to determine annual property taxes, which can be found at BCAssessment.ca. It's a rather crude calculation, which shouldn't be confused with the price a home will sell for to a willing buyer in an arm's length transaction.

Consider that the B.C. assessment is determined without an appraiser seeing the home, or asking the homeowner about its condition, such as whether any renovations have been done. How could this value be reliable without that information? Even if the province thoroughly inspected the property, values are determined annually in July, but not published until the following January. They'd still be out of date and, therefore, useless in determining a home's value six months later. To analyze fair market value for both buyers and sellers, realtors use the most recent comparable sales. Six months wouldn't be considered recent in most instances.

Now that you understand fair market value, let's discuss how realtors prepare a comparative market analysis to estimate the fair market range.

CHAPTER 8:
THE COMPARATIVE MARKET ANALYSIS – ESTIMATING THE FAIR MARKET RANGE

Realtors don't (and can't) know your home's fair market value before we list the property. We need a thorough, repeatable, research-based way to estimate the fair market range. When property values are based on what can be built on the land, or for its natural resources, rather than the home as it is, there are different ways to estimate the value. For the vast majority of our clients who are selling residential real estate, the process we use is called the Comparative Market Analysis, so we'll focus on that method of estimating value.

In this chapter, you'll

- Learn how realtors use a Comparative Market Analysis (CMA) to determine the expected price range for a home

- Discover why sellers need to understand the estimated fair market value, and how it influences their decisions during the home-selling process

- Become familiar with the key elements of a CMA

- Discuss to what degree the CMA is subjective and which factors influence the accuracy of the analysis

Your realtor uses the CMA method to determine the price range they expect your home to sell for once it's been properly marketed. Together, the sale prices of similar homes that recently sold in your neighbourhood (called comparables), along with broader statistics that indicate the speed and direction of the market, validate the price range you can reasonably expect to achieve at any given time.

Once you and your agent understand your home's approximate fair market value, you can decide whether a sale price in that range would be acceptable to you, and whether it would allow you to reach your goal with the sale. It's important to note that this range is an estimate; it's still subjective. No two homes are exactly alike, buyers and sellers have different motivations, and market conditions change over time – sometimes quite rapidly. These factors can influence the accuracy of your market value estimate.

Most people want to sell their home for as much money as possible. After all, you may be using those funds to buy another home and you need to reach a certain price to make your next move. Or, you may have other plans for those funds. Whatever the reasons, it's natural to want to maximize your sale price.

You could, of course, choose the same number you need for a planned purchase, but it will rarely match the fair market value – and that's what a buyer is willing to pay for it. Both listing and buying agents will access the same market data to create a CMA. Knowing what a buyer will likely consider fair market value sets a realistic expectation for what you can achieve.

What are the elements of a comparative market analysis?

In the CMA, your agent compares your home with current active and recently sold homes that are as similar to yours as possible. Your agent may also include expired or cancelled listings, so you can see listed homes that failed to sell, and at what prices. You'll receive this data and accompanying explanations in a written report, which you'll review with your agent.

In order to compare your home to others in your area, your agent has to learn as much about it as possible. The more thoroughly we research your home, the better the comparisons will be, leading to a more accurate estimate of fair market value.

Home viewing

First, your agent needs to view your home and tour it with you. They'll ask you to outline any renovations and maintenance you've completed while you've owned the home, and your knowledge of any upgrades that were completed before you bought it. They may also ask what materials were used. For example, "is this a hardwood floor or a really good laminate? Are the window frames wood or vinyl, and when were they installed?"

Your agent will ask other questions like, "what do you typically do in this room?" Or, "it must be bright here in the morning with that big, east-facing window?" Your agent should also notice features that might negatively affect your home's value, such as a condo located directly above the parkade gate, or a view of the power pole in the lane.

Your agent will consider your property's features, both beneficial and less attractive, to compare apples to apples in the analysis. You can further help your realtor by sharing what you love about your home. Your agent knows the market and prepares these CMAs regularly, but *you know your home*. Little things can help to establish value and enhance how we market and sell a home: Do hummingbirds visit your garden? Can you see the mountains or city lights when the leaves fall? What are your neighbours like? Can you hear them through the walls or ceiling? What's wonderful about your home that may not be readily apparent to your agent?

As a homeowner, it's natural to love your home and focus on its best features as you work with your realtor to determine its fair market value range. I suggest you consider and share what you know about your home that may be less attractive to buyers, too.

Ensuring you and your agent fully understand your home's features and benefits allows you to choose the most appropriate properties for comparison and more accurately estimate the fair market value.

Current active listings

Your agent will search to find listed properties that are similar to your home. Criteria such as age, size, location, and the number of bedrooms and bathrooms provide starting points. From a larger list, the agent will narrow the field based on what they know about different streets and buildings, whether the comparable properties are similarly renovated or updated, and other factors that affect value. Note that active listings don't reveal market value – only current list prices. These "parallel" listings help us evaluate the properties with which your home will compete for available buyers.

Sold listings

Recently sold properties that are similar to your home play the biggest role in estimating market value. Agents all access the same information, whether they represent the buyer or seller. We use the same criteria to search these sales and then to narrow the list to find the most appropriate comparable properties. Sometimes we identify a perfect comparable sale and feel quite certain about our evaluation. For example, maybe a house built in the same timeframe, on the same size lot down the street sold last month – and it was in the same condition. Or, we'll refer to the condo one floor up from yours in a newer building with the same layout.

Most comparables, however, are not perfect. A similar house did sell down the street, but it was fully renovated and yours is in original condition. Or, the same condo layout sold, but it was a year ago, and the price is out of date. In those cases, if we want to use the comparables, we have to adjust for the differences.

The sold listings are the most important part of the CMA, because they tell us not what a homeowner wanted to achieve, or their listing price, but the sale price they *actually* received.

Expired or cancelled listings

These listings can show us similar properties and prices, but because they didn't sell, we can use them to draw some conclusions. For example, if a property had professional photos and floor plans, it was listed with an experienced agent, and it sat on the market for an extended period without selling, it was probably priced too high. Maybe it provides some clues as to how we should select our list price.

Market statistics

The statistics we use as part of our CMA are divided into two categories:

Macro statistics

These are the economic conditions that factor into real estate markets, but aren't limited to them, such as interest rates, inflation, or disruptions caused by global conflict. Macro statistics are related to supply and demand, because they affect buyers' affordability and consumer sentiment. CMAs will address macroeconomic conditions at a high level by providing context, but they give more weight to local, or micro conditions.

Micro statistics

When we look at micro conditions, we consider market factors in our neighbourhood and those adjacent to it. Does the market favour buyers or sellers, as measured by the number of active listings compared to how many homes are actually selling? Are benchmark prices rising or falling? And how is the market trending if we consider a few months' worth of statistics in succession?

The sales-to-listing ratio is a valuable statistical metric in every CMA. This ratio tells us what percentage of listed homes actually sell each month, which reveals if we're in a buyer's, seller's, or balanced market.

Buyer's market – fewer than 12% of listed homes are selling in a given month. If this condition persists, it will put downward pressure on pricing.

Seller's market – more than 20% of listed homes are selling in a given month. If this condition persists, it will put upward pressure on home prices.

Balanced market – between 12% and 20% of listed homes are selling in a given month. Home prices generally remain stable when the market is balanced.

It's important for agents and sellers to understand not only what the comparables tell us about market value, but also whether market conditions are causing prices to trend up or down.

What influences the accuracy of the comparable market analysis?

Sometimes a home's final sale price doesn't land within the estimated fair market value established by the CMA. This can happen for a variety of reasons, including:

- **Time.** Perhaps you and your agent chose a list price higher than fair market value and the price failed to attract a willing buyer. By the time the price was reduced, the listing was stale.

- **An unexpected macroeconomic event** changed the market conditions either to the benefit or detriment of the seller.

- **Weak comparables.** Sometimes there isn't a truly similar home that sold recently enough to provide strong data, and your agent has to adjust the price to account for the differences. For example, a home sold nearby last week, but it was on a busier street. It was slightly smaller, had one less bathroom, no garage, and no fireplace. The more differences, the more potential for inaccuracy.

- **Bidding war.** If you chose a price on the lower end of the market range, there may have been so many buyers, or one especially motivated buyer, and that competition drove the price up.

Ultimately, pricing is still a subjective process. No two homes are exactly alike, no two sellers have the same motivation, buyers don't all have the same means, realtors have different experience and skill levels, and the market fluctuates. You and your realtor should know that a robust comparative market analysis is an excellent tool to inform your pricing strategy, while recognizing that it's simply a well-researched estimate of the market range for your home.

The CMA uses a methodology that's similar to what professional appraisers use, and it's taught in the real estate licensing program. Your agent will show you comparable listings and sales and explain why they're similar to your home. Perhaps you've viewed some of them yourself at open houses, or while visiting with a neighbour, and can also provide feedback.

Together, you can arrive at a useful estimate of market value that informs your list price strategy. Remember, we don't know the true fair market value until a home sells. The estimate you and your agent make, based on the CMA, is an important factor, but not the only one we consider when choosing your list price.

CHAPTER 9:
PRICING STRATEGIES FOR SELLERS

Many years ago, I listed a three-bedroom condo in a newer Vancouver building. The unit was a rarity: It was the only three-bedroom suite in the building and it had a beautifully landscaped patio the size of a typical backyard. The fair market value range I provided to my clients was larger than I usually offer because of the property's special features; nothing like it had recently sold.

The sellers worked well with me to prepare and stage their home. We priced it near the top of our fair market range, knowing we had a unique and special offering. We marketed it to the fullest for 10 days, set a date and time to review offers, and received four separate offers. One was below our asking price, two were slightly over, and one stood out at 14 per cent over our asking price. Again, that was 14 per cent above the top of our estimated fair market value range.

My clients were thrilled to accept the highest offer. The buyer wanted three bedrooms so her grandchildren could spend the night, and she specifically wanted to buy in this building, because it was within walking distance to her husband's care home. My client's home was literally the only newer, three-bedroom condo in close proximity to her husband. The buyer knew she was in competition, and she didn't want to lose the property.

This is the perfect example of a sale price we couldn't have anticipated: the buyer was uniquely motivated and had the means to pay a price that wasn't necessarily supported by the comparable sales.

In this chapter, we'll

- Explore the distinction between list price and sale price and the different pricing strategies that real estate agents employ
- Recognize the potential advantages and risks associated with each pricing strategy
- Discuss how to mitigate the risks by aligning the price with market conditions and property desirability

When pricing your property for sale, it's important to remember that list price is not the same as sale price. Sometimes they align, but usually, these are different numbers. Price is one of the four Ps of marketing, whether you're selling homes, pencils, or cars. The price is one part of the full marketing plan, which encourages potential buyers to attend an open house or make an appointment to view it, and ultimately, to make an offer.

We've covered a lot about fair market value because it's integral to buyers and sellers, but it begs the question: Can you choose to price your property higher and hope to achieve a sale price well above fair market value? The short answer is, yes. You can list for whatever price you choose.

Technically, you can't sell for higher than fair market value. Assuming you market the property fully and sell in an arm's length transaction, that sale price becomes, by definition, fair market value. However, you can sometimes sell for more than your realtor's analysis shows is possible, due to the subjectivity of the CMA process, rapidly changing market conditions, or a bidding war that drove the most motivated buyer to pay a higher price than comparable sales might support.

Of course, if the final sale price can be greater than your agent's market value analysis, it's equally possible that offers might come in low, or not at all. It's impossible to know exactly how the market will align with your research until the deal is done and the paperwork is signed.

As a seller, you should understand the pros and cons of different pricing strategies so you can express your preferences to your realtor. After all, this is an incredibly important part of your home's overall marketing plan. Knowing from the outset what to expect gives you context. When an offer does come in, you're in a better position to decide whether to counter or to accept it.

Once you and your realtor have used the comparative market analysis to establish and estimate fair market value for your property, there are three pricing strategies you can use to attract buyers and achieve the price you want:

1. Price above market value to leave room for negotiation

2. Price within market value range

3. Price below market value to encourage more potential buyers and, therefore, multiple offers

All three strategies have their place, so let's address the pros and cons of each, using examples of when each might be appropriate.

1. Price high to leave room for negotiation

You might use this approach when you believe a potential buyer may want to deduct money from the list price, based on a perceived issue with the home. For example, maybe you have a condo in a solid building, but it needs a full interior renovation. Buyers may want to purchase it at the right price, but not overpay, given the work required.

By pricing a little higher, you're sending a message that your condo is worth more because the building is in good condition. Once it's renovated, it will be a great home. This strategy also works with unique homes – those that might be extremely attractive to the right buyer, but wouldn't necessarily work for a more typical buyer. Sometimes, leaving room for the buyer to negotiate is a sound strategy.

The risk? Buyers don't come to see it, or those who do fail to make an offer. They don't believe the property value matches your list price. The first week on the market is critical, because this is typically when most buyers will visit your home, make competing offers, and pay full or higher than list price. The longer your home sits on the market, the less chance you'll achieve a higher sale price. You don't get a second chance to capitalize on the attention your home can attract during its first week on the market.

2. Price at fair market value

This is the Goldilocks of pricing strategies. It feels good to both agents and homeowners because it's straightforward, honest, and works for any property, in any market. In the best-case scenario, your price is reasonable, the market is strong, and you still attract more than one offer, in which case you may sell for more than your list price.

It's also possible that a fair market value price yields just one offer. When the comparables support your list price, you can negotiate a matching sale price – or a result that's close enough to satisfy your goals.

The third possibility is that your right-priced home takes a little more than a week to receive an offer. Your realtor can still negotiate and achieve full list price, or very close to it, as long the comparables support your numbers and the market hasn't dramatically slowed, putting downward pressure on prices.

The main risk here is missing the frenzy that a lower price can create. You may leave some money on the table. The property may not sell as quickly, either, which matters more to some sellers than to others, for a variety of reasons.

3. Price below your market value estimate in an effort to spark a bidding war

This strategy is often used in busy markets that favour sellers. It's the approach a realtor has used when you see a headline like, "*Home sells for $500K over asking price.*"

In this case, the buyer probably didn't lose their mind and offer $500,000 over fair market value. Instead, the seller and their agent priced the home $400,000 below their fair market value estimate, 43 buyers wrote offers, and one highly motivated buyer paid $100,000 over the estimate. The final sale price exceeded what the other two pricing strategies might have achieved. And this is why pricing low to attract multiple offers is a popular approach in a seller's market.

A sharp price is often effective in markets where buyers and agents are accustomed to bidding wars. For example, Greater Vancouver typically favours sellers because of our low supply of homes and the near-constant demand. It works well with single-family homes, where fair market value is easier to ascertain. Using lot size, property age, renovations, and layout, we can quickly find comparable properties. The scarcity of land is also enticing to many buyers. We're confident in a busy market that if we choose to price low, the market will respond in a predictable fashion, and the bet will pay off.

The risk to this approach is that if you list below your estimated market value range and you end up with just one offer, or even two at full price, you still haven't met your expectations. The buyers didn't offer over your asking price. Then you're left with less-than-ideal choices, such as:

- Work with the offers (or one of the offers), negotiate for the best price possible, and accept the result – even though it isn't what you hoped for. You may feel like a higher list price could have nudged you into a higher sale price.

- Don't accept an offer. Wait for a more motivated buyer, or multiple buyers, to come along. But remember – the offers you receive during the first week represent your best chance at a bidding war. If you price low, set an offer date, and the frenzied competition doesn't materialize, it becomes increasingly less likely to happen at all.

- Take your home off the market for a period of time and re-list closer to the price you want to achieve.

The key risk associated with pricing low is that it doesn't work and you leave money on the table. That's why it's important for your agent to fully understand the market conditions and the desirability of your property, given those conditions. If the market is hot, your property is desirable, and you have a high degree of certainty about your estimated value, this strategy should succeed. When it doesn't, it means you misjudged one of those three factors in some way, or something happened to shift the market abruptly. You're left in an unfortunate, but not fatal position.

Pricing paradox

While it's good to consider each of these pricing strategies, in Greater Vancouver and much of B.C., pricing high to leave room to negotiate is the approach least likely to achieve the highest price. Why? I believe the two main reasons are rooted in human psychology:

1. Buyers are accustomed to competing against multiple offers for the home they want. Most of the time, these markets heavily favour home sellers due to low housing supply. So, when they see a list price, they automatically assume they'll have to pay over asking. If they don't see the value at or above asking, they simply rule it out.

2. Humans have an inherent desire for social proof. Buyers become more interested in a property when they know others want it, too. Time and again, we see buyers in

competition paying a price well above what the comparable, recent home sales support. With a list price above your agent's well-researched opinion of market value, you greatly reduce your odds of receiving more than one offer. That leaves your buyer standing alone asking, "Why does no one else want to buy this home? What am I missing?"

Regardless of the strategy you choose, and what scenario you find yourself in, you never have to take an offer you don't find acceptable — even if the offer is full price or more, or if you believe fair market value has been offered. You always have choices. This can be an uncomfortable conversation with your realtor, but assuming you've built trust with a skilled professional, they will support whatever decision you make.

***

A couple of years ago, I worked with a young family who was upsizing from a townhome to a detached home. We went through a detailed CMA process and decided on the range we expected the home to sell for. After some discussion, it became clear that these clients wanted to sell for a higher price than fair market value, based on comparable sales.

I acknowledged that, in their case, the CMA was more subjective than usual; their property had some unique characteristics and there weren't any perfect comparables. This gave us some uncertainty, but it was also an advantage, because no other realtor could find a comparable to disprove that our list price represented fair market value.

My clients chose the first pricing approach: price high to leave room to negotiate.

They understood that the property might not sell quickly, there was a risk that the market could slow, and chances were slim that we'd see a first-week bidding war.

Sure enough, the home remained on the market for almost four months — an extremely long time for Vancouver real estate. During that time, we had two offers that didn't come together on price, and many other interested parties who failed to see the value reflected in the list price.

Finally, a buyer came along who did see the value. He lived nearby and wanted to stay in the neighbourhood. He was downsizing, and the home he was selling was far more valuable than the home we were selling, so price wasn't his top priority. We sold the home at full price (well over our market value estimate), giving the sellers what they needed to buy their next home.

This pricing strategy isn't suitable for most homes, because buyers rarely offer on properties they feel are overpriced. Most sellers don't want the inconvenience of spending three to four months on the market, either. But the combination of a rare home and patient sellers created an opportunity that paid off for my clients.

Bottom line: list price is a significant part of marketing a home. Price the property too low and you risk leaving money on the table. Price it too high and you risk losing the impact of that all- important first week on the market, and the potential for a strong offer or a bidding war.

You need a realistic estimate of fair market value, based on your realtor's market knowledge, recent sales, and active listings in order to make an informed decision. Knowing the three pricing strategies and the pros and cons of each puts you in an excellent position to choose the best strategy to achieve the highest price and a smoother sales process.

An offer you can (and should) refuse

Hello!

Have you been thinking of selling your home? If so, we're here to help.

No matter the reason:
- Looking to downsize
- Getting ready to retire
- Yard is too much work
- Too much clutter

Our simple stress-free process could be right for you.
Don't let the fear of selling hold you back.
Enjoy the lifestyle you deserve.

Call us today and setup an obligation-free consultation with you and your family.

If you live in a detached house, you've probably received several of these letters over the years. This company is offering to buy my house in what they call a "simple, stress-free process."

I wanted to find out what they meant, so I called them. They asked me how much I wanted for my house, and when I didn't answer, they asked that same question at least two more times.

I said I wasn't necessarily in a rush to sell, and I didn't know what my home was worth, but that I received their letter and was curious about what they'd offer. They said they'd call me back tomorrow with a dollar figure for a "cash offer."

When they called back, they offered me almost 15 per cent less than my estimate of fair market value. Real estate fees vary, but I've never heard of an agent charging anywhere near 15 per cent, so I would lose a lot of money by selling to them.

Companies like this are counting on three things:

1. You don't know what your home is worth

2. You don't know what your realtor will charge you

3. You don't know that while there's some work involved in listing your home for sale, a great realtor will help you manage and mitigate that effort

This strategy is a numbers game. If companies send out 50,000 flyers, one or two homeowners are so afraid to engage with the public sales process – or are so adverse to paying a realtor – that they'll sell at a significant discount. These sellers probably don't know how much money they're losing.

Letters like this one are, at best, a waste of paper. At worst, they're predatory. If you receive one, send it straight to the recycling bin.

Focus on buying

*L*ike weddings, graduations, landing a new job, or welcoming a child, buying a home is one of life's most memorable moments. Whether it's your first or your fifth, buying a home is incredibly exciting, because it affects so much more than where you lay your head at night. Finding a home that supports the life you want is a rewarding journey. This section explores steps you can take to prepare for a purchase, how to choose the home you want, thoughts on presale versus resale, and how you'll work with your agent to view and evaluate properties in order to find and secure the right one.

In this chapter, we'll

- Explore the elements buyers need to have in place before starting the home-buying process

- Differentiate between general affordability estimates and a formal mortgage pre-approval

- Discuss the concept of rate holds and their implications in the home-buying process

CHAPTER 10:
LENDERS AND THE BUYER'S
AGENCY AGREEMENT

*B*efore you tour potential homes, it's crucial to get your ducks in a row. You'll start by establishing essential details such as affordability, mortgage pre-approval, and ensuring the availability of deposit funds.

As a buyer, it's generally unhelpful to tour homes with your agent before:

- You know what you can afford

- You've qualified for a mortgage

- You've explored current interest rates

- You know whether you have the appropriate deposit funds

Gather your financial information and consult with a mortgage lender. Knowing how much you're qualified to spend sets a realistic budget for your home search and ensures you're not wasting time viewing homes you can't afford. Exploring homes that are outside your price range can also create unrealistic expectations and make the process more difficult.

The first step for most buyers is to choose a realtor, which we covered earlier. During the interview process, you ask questions to determine the agent's skill and service, but you'll also share what you know about your wants and needs in a new home, your budget, purchase timeline, and more. These conversations lay the foundation for what comes next.

The second step is to choose a lender for financing. Common types of mortgage lenders include traditional banks, credit unions, and mortgage brokers. Your choice of lender is important, for one obvious reason, and perhaps one that isn't as apparent. The interest rate you're offered is a consideration, and most people know this will vary. The level of service you can expect is another, perhaps less obvious factor. I suggest hiring a mortgage specialist, rather than simply working with a bank, where you might be assigned to a generalist who works 9-5, Monday through Friday.

A specialist can be an independent mortgage broker, who has access to most of the big banks and other lending institutions, or it can be an experienced mobile mortgage specialist who works with one of the major banks or credit unions. Their expertise and willingness to work outside of business hours, if required, is an important distinction.

Real estate deals are often done on evenings and weekends, and occasionally you need to reach your lender quickly to move forward with a purchase decision. Someone who specializes in mortgages, and is committed to helping their clients succeed, can be an important ally and team member in the buying process.

The third step is to get pre-approved for a mortgage. The mortgage pre-approval outlines, in writing, how much you can afford in a new home. Note that an official pre-approval is not the same as checking affordability with an online mortgage calculator. These online tools can give you a rough idea of payment totals and frequency, but they're not a promise from a lender to fund your mortgage.

For a mortgage pre-approval, you must provide documentation to the lender, such as pay stubs, letters of employment, or tax records if you're self-employed. It can be more difficult to obtain a mortgage when you're self-employed, so allow time for this step. Realtors (who are usually also self-employed) know this intimately!

Sometimes people think they're qualified for a certain price based on a conversation with a lender, but if that lender hasn't carefully reviewed your documentation, it's not a true pre-approval. You can't rely on a conversation when it's time to write an offer on a property.

Ensure that your pre-approval also secures an interest rate. A rate hold is a commitment from a lender to honour a specific interest rate for a predetermined period. For example, the rate hold guarantees the interest rate offered with your pre-approval for a specific timeframe (usually 90 days and occasionally longer). When it's time to close on a property, even if interest rates have increased, you'll still be entitled to the lower rate. If rates drop, you can take a new, lower rate. In other words, you're protected from rising rates for a limited time while you shop for a home.

There are, of course, buyers who don't require a mortgage. In this case, you need to determine where the purchase funds will come from. You may need to sell stocks, or otherwise move money around so you can quickly access it when it's time to write an offer.

Regardless of whether you're financing your purchase or not, you'll most likely need to pay a deposit when your purchase offer is firm. This can be when the seller accepts your offer, or after a subject removal period, during which time you may have secured your financing and researched the property more fully. The deposit amount is typically a minimum of 5 per cent of the purchase price, so it's important to ensure you have that amount readily available in cash or a line of credit. If it's locked up in stocks or a GIC, for example, you may not be able to access it quickly, or you could face a penalty to withdraw it.

The Buyer's Agency Agreement

Just as sellers have a listing agreement, buyers sign the Buyer's Agency Exclusive Contract. It's a legally binding contract between you and your agent that protects both parties and commits you to work together for a set period of time, in a designated geographic area.

When we discussed how realtors are paid, you learned that the vast majority of buyer's agents are paid by the sellers, as outlined in their listing agreements. The exception to this general rule occurs when a seller chooses not to pay a co-operating fee to a buyer's agent. This rarely happens, but if it does, the buyer pays the buyer's agent as outlined in the buyer's agency agreement

You and your agent can negotiate terms such as timeframe, locations, and the real estate fee when you sign the agreement.

This contract includes much of the same information as the listing agreement, such as your agent's responsibility to avoid conflicts of interest, the ways in which we use and protect personal information, and more. You'll find the standard form provided by the B.C. Real Estate Association in the Resource Guide.

Unlike the listing agreement, you don't have to sign the buyer's agreement before an agent can start helping you to buy a home. Many agents currently choose to work with their buyers in absence of a written agreement. I suspect this may change as our regulatory body establishes new rules to increase consumer transparency. While you may have bought in the past without signing a written agreement with your agent, the next time you buy a home, it may be a legal requirement.

CHAPTER 11:
GETTING REAL ABOUT YOUR
MOTIVES AND DESIRED FEATURES

Most buyers come to an initial meeting with their realtor armed with a list of features and benefits they want in a new home. This is an excellent starting place, but your criteria may change during the process.

In this chapter, we'll:

- Discuss the different property types you can choose from

- Learn the importance of flexibility in adjusting home search criteria during the buying cycle, in order to get the best results

- Explore key deciding factors such as location, property condition, and building quality

- Define your priorities around must-have features versus nice-to-have features

- Weigh the pros and cons of buying a new, presale home versus a home that has been previously enjoyed

The five most common property types

While you can buy unique offerings such as float homes, mobile homes, co-ops, bare land, and acreages, we'll focus on the five most commonly sold properties in British Columbia.

1. Condos (also called freehold strata units)

When you buy a condo, you're buying your physical living space within a condo building, as well as your share of the strata corporation's assets, including common areas in the building and the land the building sits on.

Your share is determined by your unit entitlement, which is detailed in the strata plan registered at the land title office. You'll also pay a monthly maintenance fee, which is a share of the common expenses calculated by that same unit entitlement. This fee covers items such as property management, maintenance, insurance, and a monthly contribution to the contingency reserve fund, which covers future expenditures and other costs the owners are responsible for paying.

Strata corporations are governed by the Strata Property Act, which legislates that the corporations care for the physical components of the building and elect a council to enforce the strata bylaws, make day-to-day decisions, and propose bigger decisions that members vote on at special or annual general meetings.

These properties are extremely popular because they enable buyers to get into the real estate market without the high price tag of a detached home. The sheer number of condos available also make them, by far, the most traded property type in Greater Vancouver. You'll find a link to the Strata Property Act in the Resource Guide.

2. Leasehold strata units

These are similar to freehold units in that you buy the physical living space within a building and a share of the strata corporation's assets, but the strata corporation doesn't own the land the building sits on. That land is leased, and there is typically some uncertainty about what happens when the lease term expires. Will the home-owner have the ability to negotiate an extension, or not, and at what cost? If the landowner elects not to renew the lease, what is the value of the home?

This uncertainty explains why leasehold properties are often less expensive than freehold strata units, depending on the length of the lease, whether the lease is prepaid (and for how long), or whether a monthly payment is owed. Leasehold units can be more difficult to finance, depending on the details of the lease, which also puts downward pressure on their value. They're widely seen as a less desirable investment than a freehold condo, because the buyer doesn't own an interest in the land. Given that land appreciates over time, not buildings, this structure understandably gives many buyers pause.

Leasehold units don't appeal to everyone, but they're often popular with downsizers who, for example, may be selling their family home in order to pass money along to their children and buy an affordable home for themselves – sometimes in a better location than they could otherwise afford. When resale value and building equity aren't your top goals, leasehold can be an attractive option. The Lower Mainland has a variety of leasehold properties in locations near UBC, SFU, False Creek, Granville Island, Champlain Heights, and downtown Vancouver.

3. Townhomes

Townhomes are usually, but not always, strata properties. They're subject to the same legislation as other stratas, which means they should have a strata council, maintenance fees, strata bylaws, and a contingency reserve fund. However, they may work a little differently – depending on the size of the complex.

If a townhome is part of a larger condo building, it will share all those characteristics, but a smaller, 3-10 unit townhome building may not. In those cases, owners may meet far less frequently, they may not hire a management company, and they may have a much lower contingency reserve fund. A smaller reserve fund means the owners prefer to pay for capital improvements out of pocket as they arise.

A smaller townhome complex may have lower strata fees than a large condo building because owners don't pay for management and they don't have an elevator or common areas to maintain, for example, but they still share common building insurance and exterior maintenance costs. In B.C., townhome developments that aren't stratified are sometimes referred to as row houses. These are attached houses with no shared expenses, and they're not subject to the Strata Property Act.

4. Half duplexes

Few people know that duplexes fall under the same legislation as condos and townhomes – with a few differences. A strata, is a strata, is a strata. But in practice, owners of a half duplex rarely meet, enforce the standard strata bylaws, contribute to a contingency reserve fund, or pay a monthly maintenance fee. More commonly, each side prefers to maintain their part of the property as they would a detached home. They share an insurance policy and periodically work together to pay for a new roof, which are the two expenses they *do* need to split.

5. Detached homes

A detached home is a house on a plot of land with a single owner. This is by far the simplest real estate investment, with no shared ownership, but it's also the most expensive – all things being equal. The owner is solely responsible for maintenance, which is undesirable to some, but the upfront cost of a detached home is usually the greatest limitation for most buyers. Detached homes are considered the best investment in real estate because they occupy the most owned land, which appreciates over time.

A detached home on a good-sized lot can eventually be sold to a developer who may build a duplex and coach house, a multiplex, a townhome development, or even a condo building, in some cases, so the financial upside is typically higher than other property types. Throughout B.C., there's a push for more density, particularly in cities near transit hubs and as outlined in various community plans. You'll find links to some Vancouver community plans, information on the newly announced transit-oriented density areas, and the Vancouver multiplex legislation in the Resource Guide.

**

Regardless of whether you're hoping to buy a detached home, duplex, townhome, or condo, the initial search criteria – your desired features, benefits, and price range – is the necessary start of the buying cycle.

Buyers should understand that your criteria often change. Sometimes they change due to affordability. In other cases, you'll clarify your wants and needs as you view properties and realize which attributes are essential to you and which are negotiable.

I always start by asking my clients to tell me why they want to buy a home. As speaker and leadership coach Simon Sinek explains in his 2009 book, *Start With Why*, when you know your *why*, it becomes a compass. You can refer back to it when opportunities (and challenges) arise and it can help you to stay on track.

There are many good reasons to buy a home that apply to most of us, while others are quite specific. And each of us assigns different weight to those reasons. Knowing what's most important to you and why can help you better evaluate your choices along the way.

In this section, we'll talk about why and how you might narrow or broaden your search criteria during the buying cycle, and how flexibility and an open mind can help you achieve the best results.

Sometimes *what we think we want* isn't the right thing for us. If we're too focused on our plan, we can miss a great opportunity that arises in another area. Or, the thing we want isn't possible for us, and we have to compromise on our vision.

In all my years of selling real estate, I've learned that regardless of their price bracket, buyers never get absolutely everything they want. I've helped buyers find homes ranging from $500,000 to several million dollars, and there are compromises on both ends. Oprah Winfrey can probably have everything she wants. For the rest of us, there are trade-offs.

Let's start by identifying why you want to buy a home. Here are some of the possible reasons:

1. You don't like the idea of paying someone else's mortgage by paying rent for your home.

2. You long to renovate and beautify your space, and you can't fully customize a rental home.

3. You've been evicted several times, for various reasons, and you want the security of owning your own four walls.

4. You see the purchase as a stepping stone to build equity, so you can move up the property ladder and eventually buy your dream home.

5. You've received an inheritance and believe the real estate in your market tends to outperform the stock market. You see it as a smart investment.

6. You're downsizing to free up equity to fund your retirement, or to help your grown children with a downpayment.

7. You want to move into a home with your partner.

8. You're planning to have a baby and need more space.

9. You work from home and would love to see the ocean from your office.

Your reasons are just that – yours. Some buyers focus on the financial side and want to ensure they buy a property with strong potential to increase in value. Others like the idea of building equity, but lifestyle considerations win the battle. Some people are driven by aesthetics and want a beautiful home they're proud to entertain in; there's an element of status and surroundings.

It would be easy if we all fell into one clear category. But for most of us, all of these considerations come into play. You may be engaged and likely to have children, so you need more room, *and* you want a beautiful entertaining space with an ocean view. Naturally, you want in-suite laundry, a spacious patio for your morning coffee, and a solid, well-maintained building. You must have a top floor unit with vaulted ceilings and great light that doesn't get too hot in the summer. Maybe you see where I'm going with this...

Because affordability is an issue for almost all of us, you'll probably have to decide what's most important to you. Remember why you're buying, so you can weigh the benefits and drawbacks and choose a home that fits all of your needs and many, but not all, of your wants.

Prioritizing value

Imagine you're especially interested in value. You're buying a principal residence to live in, but you also expect this home will comprise a large part of your net worth. You plan to live in it for a number of years, but it isn't your forever home. In this case, you'll want to do everything you can to ensure that when you sell, the property will have gained more value than the market average.

In real estate circles, there's an understanding that we make money when we buy a property, not when we sell it. Only when we buy do we have control over the price. When we sell, we can and do influence the price (which we've discussed), but the price a buyer is willing to pay is ultimately up to them. So, what should you consider when you're buying if resale value is your top priority?

1. **Location.** Some locations are always desirable. Consider properties close to city centres, amenities, beaches or parks, and good school districts, on quiet streets.

2. **Condition.** Choosing an unrenovated home allows you to make low-cost, high-impact upgrades that, with some time and effort,

can add value to your home. Smart renovations should increase profitability when you sell, compared to buying a fully renovated home today.

3. Building quality. If you're buying an original-condition condo in an older building, make sure the building is well maintained with a good market reputation. The upgrades you make will get maximum value, because buyers won't discount their offers for a less-than-ideal building.

4. Find a diamond in the rough. We've already covered how sellers can achieve a higher price with a robust marketing strategy that includes cleaning, staging, and more. By the same logic, a property that isn't fully marketed can represent the best purchase value. Estate sales, court-ordered sales, for sale by owner, or any property that doesn't appear clean and staged can be a great opportunity for a savvy buyer who sees hidden potential.

5. Time. The longer you can hold a home before selling it, the better its value. Realtor and legal fees, property transfer taxes, and moving costs are expensive and nibble away at your equity. So, plan to spend a minimum of five years in your home. Longer is even better.

6. Floor plan. Some are just better than others. While a non-traditional layout may work for you, considering what most buyers want can protect your investment. The placement of the kitchen and living areas, bedrooms, and bathrooms can make a big difference to the desirability of a property in a buyer's eyes.

Consider the following two floor plans. Both have two bedrooms and two full bathrooms. Both are in desirable areas on Vancouver's west side.

Totals**

Main Level:	1,157 sq. ft.	Side Deck:	157 sq. ft.
		Main Deck:	90 sq. ft.
		Master Deck:	161 sq. ft.
		Total:	408 sq. ft.

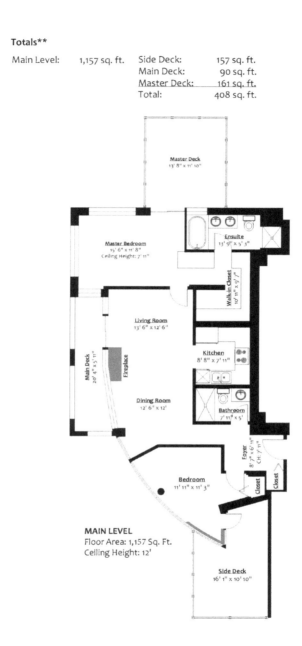

The first unit is on the penthouse level of a concrete building. It has 12-foot ceilings, air conditioning, a concierge, and ocean and city views.

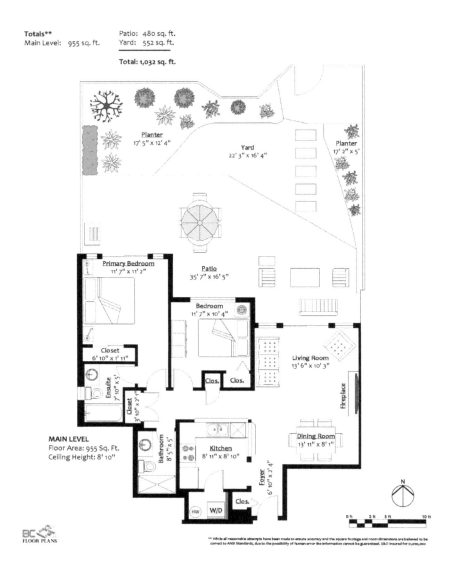

Totals**
Main Level: 955 sq. ft.

Patio: 480 sq. ft.
Yard: 552 sq. ft.

Total: 1,032 sq. ft.

Planter
17' 5" x 12' 4"

Yard
22' 3" x 16' 4"

Planter
17' 2" x 5'

Primary Bedroom
11' 7" x 11' 2"

Patio
35' 7" x 16' 5"

Bedroom
11' 7" x 10' 4"

Closet
6' 10" x 1' 11"

Living Room
13' 6" x 10' 3"

Ensuite
7' 10" x 5'

Closet
3' 10" x 2' 1"

Clos. Clos.

Fireplace

MAIN LEVEL
Floor Area: 955 Sq. Ft.
Ceiling Height: 8' 10"

Bathroom
8' 5" x 5'

Kitchen
8' 11" x 8' 10"

Dining Room
13' 11" x 8' 1"

Foyer
6' 10" x 2' 4"

HW W/D Clos.

0 ft   3 ft   5 ft   10 ft

BC
FLOOR PLANS

** While all reasonable attempts have been made to ensure accuracy and the square footage and room dimensions are believed to be correct to ANSI Standards, due to the possibility of human error the information cannot be guaranteed. E&O Insured for $1,000,000

The second unit is on the ground floor of a wood-frame building. It's almost 20 years older and has nine-foot ceilings. The condo doesn't have air conditioning, a concierge, or a view.

Both units have similar finishings, two parking spots, and lots of outdoor space.

Which would you imagine sold at a higher price per square foot? It might surprise you to learn that the older, ground-floor unit sold faster and for a higher price per square foot than the penthouse with sweeping views.

Why? Layout.

The penthouse is 20 per cent larger than the ground floor unit, but the exterior walls of the second bedroom, living, and dining spaces are rounded. Furniture placement is challenging and a significant amount of the square footage isn't practically usable.

The size and location of the fireplace is another key drawback of the penthouse floor plan. The fireplace is extremely large, and it was placed in the middle of the great room against a wall of windows. It takes up a lot of space – and it even blocks some of the view. The fireplace was also embedded in the window, so it would be costly to move or replace with a smaller model.

The penthouse kitchen is small, which is fine for buyers shopping for a studio or a one-bedroom, but most people viewing a nearly-1,200-square-foot penthouse are either buying for a couple or a small family, or they like to entertain. In all of these scenarios, the buyer would probably prefer a larger, more open kitchen to match their larger budget. Kitchens can often be renovated and opened up, but that would be a difficult task with this floor plan – if it could be done at all.

Lastly, while both units have large outdoor spaces, the first spreads that square footage over three separate patios.

By comparison, the second condo uses the space much more efficiently. The kitchen is proportionally sized for the unit and opens to the dining area, and it has a unique and highly valuable yard space for gardening and entertaining. The ground-floor unit has an excellent floor plan that appealed to more buyers – making it easier and more profitable to sell compared to the first example.

Finding value in a seller's market

Several years ago, I represented a family who wanted to move from a Mount Pleasant townhouse to their first detached house near Commercial Drive. They had two essential needs:

- The house had to be within walking distance of the elementary and high schools their children would attend.

- They wanted something they could buy for a great price and increase in value with a cosmetic renovation.

They had their eye on a house that met both criteria – and, spoiler alert, **the family was mine.**

The list price was a little higher than our fair market value estimate, but it had been on the market for a while. We thought we could negotiate a fair price. We also decided to sell our townhome before buying, because we needed to know that sale price before offering on the more expensive detached house. We listed and sold our townhome with a subject that allowed us to buy the home we wanted before finalizing the sale.

Unfortunately, the seller of our desired house was inflexible on the price. We couldn't secure a price we were willing to pay. So, we went back to the drawing board and toured every house listed in our price range, within a 10-block radius of the kids' schools.

One of the houses was located right between the two schools, less than three blocks from both. It was listed by an out-of-market agent who put the keys in a lockbox on the front door and didn't show the home in person. There was a vague description, no professional floor plan, and no interior photos. From the outside, the house looked tiny. We almost didn't view it, but we were leaving no stone unturned.

When we walked into the house, we were instantly taken by mid-century modern touches like coved ceilings, original fir floors with inlay, and a cute 1950s kitchen – none of which were evident from the online listing. But we knew we had found the one when we realized that the walk-out basement was full height. It was almost eight feet, which is a rare find in an older Vancouver home.

It was impossible to see these details from the photos or the front of the house. The property was in original but well-kept condition, with a single owner who had lived there for decades. The layout wasn't perfect, but it was workable, and we knew that with a cosmetic renovation, we could make it what we wanted. We negotiated a price well below our fair market value estimate, in part because the agent hadn't done anything to market the home and we had no competition.

Value buying means buying for the long term

For most of us, real estate purchases are a long-term investment. On average, people move every six to seven years, so consider the future when you're shopping for a home. Buy something you'll be comfortable in for several years. I often have to remind buyers that their lifestyle will not always look the same as it does right now.

For example, a young couple working downtown asks their agent to help them buy a one-bedroom condo near their offices. This seems perfectly appropriate until the agent learns they're getting married next year and they plan to start a family right away. They'll quickly outgrow a one-bedroom unit and could lose any equity they build in this home between real estate and legal fees, property transfer taxes, and moving costs when they upgrade. They'll be better off financially by purchasing something with an extra bedroom, even if they have to move a little further from the downtown core to afford it.

Families also forget that their circumstances will rapidly evolve. Parents of young children often emphasize the need to easily enter and exit their home with a stroller, for example, and forget that children quickly outgrow strollers. A couple of years of inconvenience might be worthwhile if the home checks most other boxes.

Older buyers should also consider their changing needs. Fit and healthy 70-year-olds may be comfortable buying a home that spans two or three floors, but they might want to consider a single-floor option instead. If they do want a larger home, perhaps they can buy one with a main floor bedroom and full bathroom. This layout would allow them to live predominantly on the main floor if they eventually have trouble climbing stairs.

Alternatively, a home with an extra bedroom and bathroom could enable them to host a family member or professional caregiver – allowing them to age in place. Seniors might also consider buying a home that's a short, level walk to transit, green space, and groceries, so it's easier to maintain independence and an active lifestyle. The buyer, of course, is the ultimate decision-maker. But, a good agent will challenge their client from time to time and ensure they consider details that may not be obvious to them.

There are hundreds of these different scenarios. Changing the search parameters to match your preferred price range, considering lifestyle and financial factors, can take many shapes. You may start with a plan, but you don't know exactly how it will unfold until you start – and that can be stressful.

The process of researching properties, viewing and discussing homes, making offers, and adjusting search parameters will clarify what you need in your new home, especially when you remember why you want to buy a home in the first place. Prepare for changes, but remember; you're in the driver's seat. Your agent is there to ask questions, share their expertise, challenge assumptions, and to support you, but this is your journey.

CHAPTER 12:
VIEWING PROPERTIES

*I*n this chapter, we'll explore:

- The time commitment required to shop for properties – from the initial search set-up to making an offer

- Strategies for viewing potential homes, including public open houses and dedicated tours

- The importance of an open collaboration with your real estate agent

- How to view homes that aren't contenders, but which help you to compare value and gain confidence in your choices

Once you've chosen your realtor, obtained a pre-approval and rate hold, and you have a good sense of what you want (and why), you're ready to shop for your new home. Usually, this begins when your realtor sets up an online search that automatically emails matching properties to you and your agent as soon as they're listed. The search can screen for neighbourhood, price, number of bedrooms and bathrooms, square footage, and more to find homes that most closely match your criteria.

How much time you'll devote to the process depends on a number of factors, but especially, your motivation. If you've been evicted from your rental and need a new home, you'll have a clear timeline; the clock is ticking. You might have your agent on speed dial and view properties two, three, even four days a week.

If, however, you own your home and you're interested in moving only when you find a near-perfect property, you may have a more relaxed pace. Years might elapse between the first meeting with your agent and an accepted offer.

There's no set amount of time and no typical number of homes that buyers see before making an offer. Some will see three homes and buy one. Others will shop for years before finding their dream home. There are so many variables that affect the process:

1. Are you looking for your first home?

2. Are inventory levels high or low within your preferred price range?

3. Are you looking for something unique or a more typical style of home?

4. What's your decision-making style? Do you move quickly or are you more deliberative? Are you analytical and data-driven, or will you just know?

5. How long will it take for you to find a home that checks enough boxes to write an offer?

6. Will you have to write a few unsuccessful offers before getting an offer accepted?

7. When would you like to move?

Motivated buyers like to physically see homes as soon as possible, so most agents will arrange tours of the most promising properties that come up in your search. This can be just one or two properties if listings are lean, or as many six or seven. Seeing more than this number is usually counterproductive, because it's easy to get overwhelmed and forget the details. An exception might be someone who's coming in from out of town and has a limited amount of time to see as many homes as possible. In this case, tours can be longer.

Open houses are a convenient way to see multiple homes without the pressure of set appointment times. Most are held on Saturday and Sunday from 2-4pm. However, if something great hits the market on Monday, you may want to see it earlier, for two reasons:

1. The seller may be looking at offers as they come in, so that exceptional home could be off the market by Saturday.

2. If the property ticks most of the boxes for you and looks good on paper, why not be among the first to view it? This gives you time to see it again, view it at a different time of day, and do some research before writing an offer.

Plan to tour homes two or three times a week, so you see all the options that fit your parameters. Some homes are only available to show at specific times, for example, such as a homeowner who's accommodating tenant schedules. Buyers need to be flexible.

Some people like to see homes on their own by attending open houses. They only bring their agent into the process when they're considering an offer. There's nothing wrong with going it alone, but remember; the more homes your agent sees with you, the better they get to know you and your preferences. Every tour is an opportunity for conversations that build trust and rapport – and that familiarity can be invaluable during an offer process.

Another reason to invite your realtor to see as many homes as possible? You may come across one you really love. Imagine you've attended an open house on Sunday at 3:30 pm. It's packed with prospective buyers and their agents. From what you can see, the house is a gem. You want more information, but the listing agent is busy talking to other people and doesn't have time to answer your questions.

You leave the open house and immediately call your agent, but they're hosting their own open house or touring properties with another buyer. They don't answer. Your agent calls you back within the hour, but the open house is over. Your agent sees that the listing realtor has set an offer date for the next morning. She tries to talk the listing agent into another viewing, right now, but he's already left the property and has firm dinner plans. He also tells your agent that three parties have said they'll write an offer the next morning.

If you want to make an offer, your agent will have to write it for you without first seeing the home – leaving you without the full benefit of their professional expertise, in terms of value, condition, and more. That's why I urge you to view any homes that excite you, based on the listings, with your realtor. Seeing them together primes you to act quickly, if one turns out to be a great fit.

When you see multiple properties with your realtor, you can also rule out homes that don't work for you. These viewings can demonstrate what value looks like in your price range, what's most important to you, and which features would be nice, but aren't deal-breakers. Aim to see enough homes that when you get an accepted offer, you don't wonder "what if?" You don't worry about the one that got away.

Ultimately, the home viewing process is highly personal. It varies based on how you make decisions, how well you know the neighbourhoods, whether you're an experienced or first-time home buyer, and many other factors.

Sometimes, a buyer needs just one more tour

Remember that large, two-bedroom Fairview condo I bought to share with my two roommates? Well, it almost slipped away after an exhaustive search. I had viewed about 40 homes, offered on two and lost them in multiple offers, and almost offered on a home that wouldn't have worked well. You would think I had learned enough to feel confident in my choice. But, once I had an accepted offer and was doing my due diligence, I wondered if this really was the one. I worried that once I firmed up this deal, a better home might come on the market.

My realtor, Dale, listened patiently to my concerns. He was *especially* patient considering all we'd been through, how close we were, and that my hesitation was about to blow it. "I like this property for you, Mary," Dale said calmly. "But it doesn't matter whether *I* like it."

He wanted to ensure I wouldn't suffer buyer's remorse or walk away from a great decision. So, Dale suggested we go on one more epic tour – viewing every two-bedroom condo in Fairview that we hadn't yet seen, including several that came on the market that week. After considering everything out there, I realized that none came close to my chosen property. That last, generous tour gave me the confidence to move forward and never look back.

You'll have a better experience, and get more value from your realtor, if you devote significant time and attention to the process. Lean on your agent from the beginning. When markets favour sellers, homes sell quickly and buyers must be decisive. View as many homes as you need to feel confident in your choice, knowing this number will depend on market conditions and your decision-making style.

You may need to see 50 homes, or you may need to see three. When a property interests you, go for a second visit, walk the neighbourhood at different times of the day, and talk to friends and family. Do whatever you need to envision what your life would be like in a particular space before you make an offer. Your agent would rather see you lose a home or two as you learn what's important to you than buy the wrong home because you felt pressure to act before you were ready.

CHAPTER 13:
THE OFFER

When you've found a home you love and you've done just enough research on the property to take the next step, it's time to write an offer. Let's cover the basics, including:

- How to determine an appropriate offer price
- Common subject clauses, also known as conditions, used in real estate contracts, such as financing, document review, and home inspections
- Strategies to make an offer more attractive during a bidding war, such as price, subject clauses, due diligence, and a personal touch

In the context of purchasing a home, an offer is the written proposal a potential buyer makes to the seller, outlining the terms and conditions under which the buyer is willing to purchase the property. This document serves as the foundation for negotiations between the buyer and seller.

The offer typically includes key details, such as:

Offer price: The amount the buyer is willing to pay for the property.

Subject clauses: Conditions that must be met for the offer to proceed.

Closing date: The date on which the buyer expects to complete the purchase and take possession of the property.

Inclusions and exclusions: A list specifying which items are included or excluded from the sale, such as furniture, lighting, garden items, and more.

Terms and conditions: Any additional terms or conditions the buyer wishes to include, such as repairs or specific requests related to the sale.

Your agent will have the standard Contract of Purchase and Sale form used exclusively in British Columbia for resale properties. Like the standard listing contract, it's a boilerplate document written by lawyers, with negotiable sections such as the offer price, dates, and subjects.

You'll find the British Columbia Real Estate Association standard Contract of Purchase and Sale form in the Resource Guide, along with a document explaining its terms and conditions.

Once the offer is submitted, the seller has the option to accept, reject, or change some of the key terms and counter the offer. If the seller accepts the offer as-is, the parties move forward to finalize the sale. If there's a counter-offer, negotiations continue until both parties reach an agreement or decide to walk away. It's essential for buyers and sellers to carefully review and understand the terms of the offer, because if both sides accept it, the offer becomes a contract that binds both parties.

As a buyer – particularly when the market is brisk – you're asked to make highly consequential decisions in a short time. The more you understand how this process unfolds in different circumstances, the better prepared you'll be for the moment these decisions are made.

Let's now discuss the various circumstances that can arise when you submit an offer.

For the moment, let's assume you're writing an offer on a property, and at present, no one else has indicated they'll also be writing. You're expecting to enter a one-on-one negotiation with the seller. Note that we'll cover the art of negotiation in the next section.

How much will you offer for the home?

Remember that the list price isn't necessarily the fair market value of a home. The list price is a marketing tool meant to attract buyers and elicit this very moment – your decision to write an offer. So, if the list price is a marketing tool, and not the home's value, how do you determine the value?

You guessed it: a comparative market analysis, as we covered earlier. The same process a listing agent uses to advise a seller on list price is the process your agent will use to determine a fair price for your chosen home. Remember that these values are somewhat subjective, and it's common for the agent representing the buyer to take a slightly different view on the market and comparable properties.

Once the CMA is complete and you and your agent have determined your target price range, you can decide what price you want to write in your initial offer:

- Should you be straightforward and write your final price, telling the listing agent, "this is our offer based on our reading of the current market – take it or leave it?"

- Or should you start a little lower, leaving room for negotiation?

There's simply no correct answer. We don't have enough information. We'll cover negotiation in more detail later on, but for now, we've used the CMA to determine the market value range, which directly informs our offer price.

What are subject clauses? Which are the most common? And how long is a typical subject, or due diligence period?

Subject clauses are conditions written into a purchase contract that can benefit a buyer or seller. Most commonly, they benefit buyers. Subject clauses allow buyers to secure a property and give them time to complete their due diligence.

Typical subject clauses include:

- **Subject to financing**. While a buyer is pre-approved for a mortgage before writing an offer, this pre-approval is contingent upon the bank's satisfaction with the property itself. That's why a "subject to financing" clause is important if you're borrowing to fund your purchase.

- **Subject to document review**. These include a title search, Property Disclosure Statement, oil tank certificate, strata documents, and all the other information we'll cover in the due diligence section.

- **Subject to home inspection**. This subject enables the buyer to secure a visual property inspection performed by a licensed home inspector who provides a written report.

These are the three most common subject clauses we include for our buyers' protection when writing an offer. There are countless others, such as a subject to obtaining a satisfactory insurance rate, subject to sale, and subject to confirming the allowance for a building scheme, per the city.

How long does the subject period last?

The subject term is negotiable. It can range from one day, if you believe you can quickly get the information you need, to several months in the case of a land purchase – if you need to confirm that the city would permit your building plans, for example. Most contracts provide 5-10 business days to remove the three most typical subjects. This is more than enough time for a standard document review, home inspection, and financing – assuming the buyer is already pre-approved for the mortgage amount.

Making an offer when you're competing with other buyers

In a busy seller's market, buyers often find themselves competing for properties. It's a common theme throughout this book, because this situation is unavoidable. Many Canadian markets don't have enough homes to satisfy potential buyers. This structural imbalance changes the rules of the game.

B.C. listing agents are required to inform buyer's agents whether or not they're in competition. For most buyers, a multiple offer situation affects their offer price, some terms and subject clauses, and the time period they need to perform their due diligence.

Buyers who know they're competing for a home may also choose to include a personal letter with a photo of themselves, their pets, or their children to (hopefully) endear themselves to the home-owner. It may seem like wishful thinking to believe this extra step could influence a complete stranger, but I can tell you from experience that it can make the difference between an accepted offer – or the chance to revise your offer – and a lost opportunity.

Home sellers and their agents are human, after all. A well-executed offer that includes this personal touch sends a message that the buyer loves a home enough to do everything they can to secure it. As long as it's thoughtful and well-written, I've never found that it hurts a buyer's prospects.

When you're in competition, there's no expectation that the seller will give you a counteroffer. So, many buyers will write their best offer price, rather than an opening bid to start the conversation.

To make your offer more attractive to the seller, you may also choose not to include certain subjects. For example, you may choose to read all the documents ahead of the offer date, so you don't need that subject clause in the offer. You may also choose to inspect the home before the offer date for the same reason. A financially secure buyer – one who's buying below their means – may also choose to forego the subject to financing clause.

Some lenders will also evaluate the home ahead of time to ensure your chosen property will be approved. This is one of the reasons why I encourage clients to choose a mortgage specialist; someone who offers a high level of service and will answer their phone after 5pm on offer day.

A buyer who can write a no-subject offer stands a much better chance of winning the home in competition. That's why performing your due diligence before writing an offer can be a good strategy.

The downside? You'll spend a lot of time reviewing documents, working with your lender, and inspecting a property that you may not win in a bidding war. You could also spend $500-1,000 on a home inspection for that lost property. But, this could also happen when you're the sole buyer for a home that fails an inspection. In a competitive market, many buyers are willing to do their home-work before the offer period, because it gives them stronger odds of winning the home they want.

In B.C., listing agents are required to inform buyer's agents when they're in competition and provide a written record (within 24 hours) stating the number of offers received and which brokerages submitted the offers. The province established this requirement in 2024 to give buyers peace of mind. If a listing agent claims the buyer is in competition, they have to supply written documentation. In short, they have to prove it.

CHAPTER 14:
BUYER BEWARE – PERFORMING
YOUR DUE DILIGENCE

*I*n this chapter, we'll explore:

- What buyers need to understand about a property they want to purchase

- The joint responsibility of buyers and their agents when researching properties, and how you can work together to learn as much as possible about a home before you buy it.

We toured the home and we love it! Now what?

It's a great day when you find an affordable home in your preferred location that you love enough to consider buying. Between that moment and a firm deal on the home, there's a lot of work to do. You need to evaluate the property for details that may not be readily apparent, such as:

- Are there any issues with water ingress?

- How old are the windows? Are they double-paned and performing well, or are the seals broken?

- How old is the roof? Is it leaking or compromised in any way?

- How is the home heated? Is this system functioning well? Is it energy efficient? How much does it cost to heat and cool?

- Is there an underground oil tank on the property (especially relevant to older homes)?

- How is the property zoned? How does that affect land value? Will the street character change in the near future?

- Is there a current or past pest infestation?

- Is the electrical system up to current code? Or is it composed of old knob and tube or aluminum wiring?

- Are the pipes made of copper, PEX, or poly-B – and why does the material matter?

- Does the property have any rights of way or encroachments on or by a neighbouring home?

- Were renovations done with permits, and if not, what are the risks? How do they affect the home's value?

These are just some of the questions you'll want to answer before you proceed. Details such as electrical, plumbing, and the age of the roof can all affect your home insurance rates – or even your ability to secure insurance at all. Others may determine whether the property is suitable for your lifestyle, both now and in the future. These questions can usually be answered, to a reasonable degree, during the due diligence period with a combination of city records, documents provided by the homeowner, inspections by a licensed home inspector, and other service providers.

Taking the time to investigate a property is important, because most buyers will purchase a resale home, which has been previously enjoyed and isn't being sold by a developer. These homes don't usually come with a warranty. If the home is new enough to have some warranty left, it may not cover what you want it to. A resale home isn't being sold by a builder or a big company, but another person, just like you. They probably have little construction expertise and have no obligation to turn their home over to you in any particular condition, except the condition it was in when you saw it.

It's essential for you and your agent to learn as much as you can about a property before you're locked into the purchase, so you:

- Know what you're signing up for, in terms of future maintenance or repair costs

- Feel confident about the price you're paying for the home, considering its condition and all other factors

There are many documents that you and your agent will try to obtain and review. The following relate to all property types:

1. Property Disclosure Statement

The seller completes this document by answering a list of standard questions about their home, such as the age of the roof, whether renovations were performed without permits, the presence of pests, and more. It's important to note that all questions are answered **to the seller's knowledge**.

Sellers are not expected to have specialized knowledge about electrical, plumbing, and other technical details. They aren't required to investigate the age of the roof, for example, if they haven't replaced it while they owned the property. Sellers are required to answer questions honestly, but you should view this disclosure as a first step. You'll need to follow up by seeking answers from professionals or finding them in other documents, such as service receipts.

2. City permits

These documents outline city-approved renovations, gas hookups, electrical upgrades, and more. They also tell you whether the permit is complete, or closed, or the city still requires further inspections. Recent permits can be found online, but you'll need to obtain older permits from the current homeowner, or from a municipality or district through a multi-step process that requires some time and money.

In Vancouver, the market moves quickly and buyers don't always have time to get all the documents they might want, especially when there are other buyers for a desirable home. Many homes have had renovations completed without city permits. Buyers need to decide whether any unpermitted renovations or missing documents are essential to their confidence and comfort level.

3. Title search

In B.C., sellers are required to provide buyers with a current title search. This document outlines whether there's a mortgage registered on the property and can include other useful information such as liens or other charges, encumbrances, rights of way, and more. If there's something of concern on the title, you can seek legal advice. Some realtors provide this information for their clients at no extra cost.

4. Home warranty insurance

Most newly built homes in the U.S. and Canada come with a builder's warranty.

You may also be able to obtain other documents, such as natural gas and other energy bills, property tax bills, radon or EnerGuide ratings, and more.

Additional documents specific to detached homes

1. Oil tank certificate

Underground oil tanks were commonly used to heat homes in the early-to-mid-1900s. In some cases, homes have been renovated with a new heating source, but those old tanks remain under the lawn, patio, or even under an addition to the home. This can lead to problems if oil remains in these tanks. Over time, tanks can corrode and leak, requiring expensive remediation.

In most cases, the listing agent hires a professional to scan the property for an underground oil tank and provides that certificate to potential buyers. There are, however, limitations to this process; many providers use a scanner that can't penetrate concrete. If, for example, the whole backyard is paved, the scan may not give you total assurance that there isn't an oil tank underground. In that case, you'll need to decide whether you want to seek more information.

2. Survey certificate

This is the gold standard for documenting lot lines, and determining whether buildings, walkways, or fences encroach on the property, and more. Most sellers don't have this certificate readily available, so if you have questions or feel it's especially important, you may have to arrange (and pay for) a professional survey.

Additional documents for strata properties

1. Strata plan

This document provides important information, including the size of the strata unit, how parking and storage lockers are assigned or designated, the buyer's proportion of common expenses, and the buyer's proportional entitlement in the event the whole build is sold, among other details.

2. Insurance certificate

This shows you how the building is insured, and outlines which deductibles your own insurance should cover, and more.

3. At least two years' worth of strata minutes

The strata minutes provide clues about how the strata corporation functions, the decisions they've made, and what maintenance projects have been completed during that time.

4. Financial statements

Includes the annual budget, income statement, and other financial details.

5. Form B

This provides a snapshot of the unit as it relates to the building: parking spots and storage locker numbers, monthly strata fee, contingency reserve fund totals, whether the current owner owes money to the strata, and more.

6. Depreciation report

A report completed every three years that provides general information about the building, and the age and condition of the building's components. It also includes funding models the strata may contemplate to prepare for future maintenance and capital expenditures, such as new roofing, elevator upgrades, and more.

Once your agent has secured all the relevant documents, you both have a responsibility to read and understand the documents to ensure you're protected.

Usually, your agent will share the documents so you can read them independently and make notes. Your agent will highlight anything that might affect your use of the property, and answer questions that arise as you read.

Ideally, your agent will also give you a written summary highlighting the most important aspects of the building – whether it's a strata or a house – plus any red flags and items you might want to explore in more detail. Your agent should be able to put your concerns in context and help you decide whether you feel confident moving forward, or if there are enough risks associated with a property that you prefer to move on.

Home inspection

Buyers should strongly consider hiring a licensed, professional home inspector to perform a visual inspection of the property. This is usually done after you secure an accepted offer on the home subject to document review, home inspection, financing, and/or other conditions. In a strong seller's market, these inspections are often done before the set offer date, so buyers can present those clean (subject-free) offers that sellers love.

The home inspection reveals key details about the property you're considering. It also fills in gaps from the documents, such as the approximate age and condition of the roof or windows, whether there's any moisture ingress, or an insect infestation. Inspectors will sometimes find outdated and potentially dangerous materials such as asbestos, or knob and tube wiring.

The limitation of a visual home inspection is right in its name: home inspections are purely visual. You don't own the home yet, so your inspector can't remove and send chunks of drywall to a lab, and they can't drill holes to search for moisture. They won't move a heavy armoire or construction debris to access an outside wall.

Inspectors do use drones to photograph the roof and other hard-to-access areas. They have moisture readers and devices to check whether electrical outlets are grounded. The best inspectors have experience and education in building, electrical, plumbing, and use a combination of their tools and knowledge to discover whether a home was well built and maintained. They can also note potential costs for upcoming repairs or maintenance, and are well worth the $500-1,000 you'll pay for their service.

*DID YOU KNOW?

It's a good idea to inspect a home before you buy it, even if it's brand-new. Some buyers believe there's no reason to inspect a new home because:

1. It's under warranty

2. The City has signed off and, therefore, the home is built to code

A warranty is nice and covers many, but not all, deficiencies. You can avoid claiming against the warranty by hiring an inspector to find the deficiencies before the builder/seller has your money. That's when you have the most leverage.

Municipal building codes are based on the sizes and setbacks the land zoning allows. They also confirm that the property aligns with both the building plans and safety standards, but you can't rely on it to confirm quality, which varies significantly between projects.

***

Several years ago, I was working with a young family with a big budget. They were looking at west side homes on 50-foot lots, with a budget up to $10 million dollars. We saw many different houses over a six-month period, and when a brand-new home was listed in the perfect location with the right layout, my clients fell in love. They wrote an offer that was accepted, subject to the usual conditions, including a home inspection.

My clients thought that this brand-new, warrantied home signed off by city inspectors didn't need an inspection. Eventually, I convinced them to hire an inspector with an excellent reputation for attention to detail. Well, the inspection didn't go as my clients hoped. There weren't any catastrophic failures, but the inspector found a variety of substandard building practices, such as improperly caulked sinks, loose door handles, gaps in baseboards and mouldings, roof drainage deficiencies, and other exterior weaknesses.

The inspector said all these items could be mitigated, but the sheer number of visual issues were a red flag. If the exterior and finishings were so problematic, what kind of shortcuts might the builders have taken with the framing, foundation, or parts of the house he couldn't access? My clients confidently walked away from a $7-million-dollar house because of these inspection results – a decision well worth the $1,000 price tag for the inspection.

As we've discussed, most of the buyer's due diligence involves the home inspection and documentation. Some buyers are also concerned about zoning, nearby construction, environmental issues such as radon, or nearby power plants. Let your agent know your specific concerns, so they can help you find all the answers you need to make a fully informed decision to move forward or walk away.

Remember

Due diligence can occur before you make an offer, or after your offer has been accepted, assuming your offer includes a subject to document review and home inspection. You may decide to review the documentation, including the home inspection report, before you make an offer, so you don't need to include those subjects – making it more attractive to the seller. This approach is popular in Greater Vancouver, where properties often sell in multiple offers and buyers who write firm offers, without subjects, often win bidding wars.

CHAPTER 15:
BUYING A PRESALE CONDO

A presale condo is one that isn't built yet. Developers usually need to sell a portion of the building before a bank will lend the money they need to fund the project at a favourable interest rate.

Buying a presale condo is a different process than buying a resale home. The contracts and other documentation, financing arrangements, rescission period, risks, and timing are all unique. You can't view a home that doesn't yet exist, so you'll choose based on renderings, models, samples, and floor plans. It's a different experience that demands a separate discussion. And buyers, particularly investors, often ask whether it's more financially advantageous to buy a presale or resale condo.

MYTH

Presale condos are always cheaper than resale homes.

Many people mistakenly believe that presales are always a good deal, because they tend to be worth more when completed than when a buyer enters into a contract. This misconception is due to the fact that condo buildings take three to five years to build and in Greater Vancouver, prices almost always increase in a three-to-five-year span. Your presale is worth more than your contract price due to the passage of time, not because you landed a great deal when you signed the offer. A resale condo will also likely appreciate over the same time period.

The benefits of buying presale

- You get a brand-new home
- The home comes with a warranty
- The developer will fix any deficiencies in the weeks prior to completion
- You have more choices – including the layout, floor level, and orientation
- You have seven days to change your mind and cancel the contract, with no penalties
- You can park money during the construction phase without making payments
- The project may have a lending partner who guarantees your interest rate at completion, which could be lower than the prevailing rates when your mortgage begins
- If home prices rise during the construction phase, your presale can be worth more when completed than when you purchased it

The risks of buying presale

- You make decisions based on floor plans, renderings, and samples, but you can't see the finished product before you commit
- You must use the developer's purchase contract, which is written to protect them (not you) and can restrict your ability to sell the unit before completion
- The disclosure statement allows for some variance in the build, so there may be minor, yet disappointing surprises when it's completed
- The build may take longer than expected, keeping your deposit money tied up and leaving you without a home

- The quality may not meet your expectations

- The quoted strata fee is almost always lower than you can expect to pay once the strata corporation is established

- You'll pay GST on your purchase

- If market conditions favour buyers when you get the keys, your suite could be worth less at completion than when you bought it

As with almost all real estate matters, the question of whether to buy pre-construction or an existing condo is complicated. It also depends on the market and your personal circumstances.

Presale can be a great option if you're comfortable with your current living situation and your moving date is flexible, or if you're purely looking for an investment.

Several years ago, I helped an investor to buy a presale studio condo in East Vancouver. She had enough cash on hand for the developer's graduated deposit, but she was on maternity leave and wouldn't have qualified for a mortgage at that time. Securing a presale unit allowed her to put her capital to work, knowing she would qualify for financing when the project completed two years later and she was back to work as a lawyer.

In terms of value, my client made a great choice. The building was the first condo project sold in a newly rezoned area, so the pricing was attractive compared to projects that would follow. When she took ownership of her suite and rented it out two years later, the property value had increased by approximately 20 per cent. Rents in the area had increased, too. She got a great return on her investment and, to this day, the rent covers her ownership costs. It's a comfortable investment for her to hold.

Presales can be especially advantageous when your agent has a good relationship with the company marketing a new building, so you can get in early and choose your unit before the public release date. Having your choice of suites can also enable you to find a somewhat underpriced unit. Maybe it's a rooftop deck, or the top-floor corner suite; look for standout features you can capital-ize on.

Value always depends on overall market conditions. In a buyer's market, developers sell many units at once, so they may throw in a bonus to entice you to sign the contract. On the other hand, most developers are patient. They don't tend to negotiate their list prices. Compare that to a homeowner in a buyer's market who needs to sell. You may be able to negotiate and land a better price with a motivated seller than you would with a developer.

In a strong seller's market, you can't negotiate presale discounts – and you may not be able to buy at all. I've witnessed situations where securing a presale is more difficult than buying tickets to an NHL playoff game.

Keeping your options open may be the best approach. Consider presale and existing market inventory. If you can get new construc-tion and you're comfortable paying the deposit without a firm completion date, it might be a good option.

It's worth noting that even highly reputable builders can encoun-ter issues that owners need to mitigate at completion. This might involve inspections, conflict, and in the worst-case scenario, legal action. Unfortunately, buying new doesn't guarantee that you won't have any construction or maintenance issues. In B.C., there have been several high-profile cases where buildings sold for extremely high prices, yet buyers were largely disappointed by the quality of the finished product.

***

In some ways, buying a home is more complicated than selling. Choosing from the available options, deciding between pre-con-struction or current building stock, and competing for the one you want can be all-consuming. Devote your time, involve your realtor as much as possible, keep an open mind, and listen to your heart – but flex your critical thinking skills, too.

Your criteria may change as you learn about different locations, features, and values, so stay flexible. Remember why you want to buy a home in the first place, and be willing to adapt to new information. For most people, buying a home is both personally and financially rewarding, so take the time you need to make a fully informed choice – and don't give up.

Negotiating offers and closing the deal

CHAPTER 16:
NEGOTIATION TACTICS

First, let's acknowledge how much we've covered: what to look for in an agent, the role of the lender, how homes are marketed and sold, the steps involved in buying a home, common industry contracts, and so much more.

All this leads us to perhaps the most important aspect, and the number-one skill you need from a realtor: negotiation.

If you're human, you have negotiating skills. We negotiate every day – with our kids, our partners, service providers, friends, teachers, and bosses.

But real estate negotiations are tough, in terms of their complexity and both the financial and emotional stakes. How your realtor frames the negotiation and applies proven strategies and techniques can dramatically affect your results.

You might wonder why it's important for you, as the client, to understand this part of the process. After all, you won't be negotiating with realtors on the other side of the transaction. Yet, knowing how your realtor interacts with other agents – and what they need from you – enables you to collaborate with your realtor to achieve the results you want.

The challenge of real estate negotiations

In their book, *Getting to Yes*, authors Roger Fisher, William Ury, and Bruce Patton define negotiation as "a back-and-forth communication designed to reach an agreement when you and the other side have some interests that are shared and others that are opposed."

Real estate negotiations are complex. They involve many factors, including:

- The negotiation styles and skill levels of the agents representing both the buyer and the seller

- Negotiators who know their own clients, but have limited knowledge of the objectives, means, and personality of the principal on the other side of the transaction

- Buyer and sellers who tend not to be expert negotiators, but are the ultimate decision-makers

- Agents who don't know each other and haven't established trust

- Agents who do know each other and haven't established trust

- Buyers and sellers who can be highly emotional during negotiations

- High stakes that can elicit anxiety among buyers, sellers, and even inexperienced agents

Sources of negotiating power

Buyers and sellers come into negotiations with circumstances that give them power. This is sometimes called your negotiating position. Knowing where your power comes from enables you to take steps to increase it, such as gathering more information about the other party. A realistic understanding of your bargaining power guides the decisions you'll make during the negotiation.

Three types of power in real estate negotiations include:

1. Market power

Do the statistics show that you have an advantageous market position? For example, are you selling a house in a sought-after neighbourhood, where the rare listed homes sell quickly at strong prices? Or are you selling an investment condo in a large building with 21 other units currently on the market? We can't control whether our market power is low or high.

2. Alternatives or BATNA

What is your plan B if this offer doesn't come together? For example, if you're the buyer, are you renting a home nearby, so you can simply wait for the next one? Or have you been evicted from your home and need to move out in four weeks?

BATNA stands for **Best Alternative To a Negotiated Agreement**. If your best alternative to a proposed deal is extremely unattractive, you have low BATNA. At the time of negotiation, there isn't much you can do to improve it. But, remember our discussion about whether it's better to buy or sell your home first. Buying first can put you in a disadvantageous position when you're negotiating the sale of your home, because you're probably motivated to sell in order to avoid carrying both mortgages. That's an example of low BATNA.

3. Information power

Understanding your power and needs, the macro and micro data influencing market prices (CMA), property details, the other agent's negotiating style and experience, and the other party's motivation, BATNA, and budget can increase your power. You can boost your agent's informational power by being open and honest about what's most important to you, but it's your agent's preparation and experience that will give them more information than the agent on the other side of the transaction.

*PITFALL ALERT

Withholding information – such as your financial position or motivations – from your realtor in an effort to control a negotiation is rarely the best strategy. By this point in the buying or listing process, you should have built a strong sense of trust with your agent. They're the expert negotiator, so tell them everything; you can decide together what to use in the negotiation and what to hold back.

Negotiating position versus interest

Skilled negotiators know the difference between arguing positions and interests, and will choose the right tool for the situation. This can be a huge advantage to you, and the difference between landing a good deal or a bad deal – or even reaching an agreement at all.

Imagine you're the seller and this is your position: "I won't take less than $1 million dollars for my house."

Your interest is slightly different: "I need $1 million dollars from my house to afford the home I have my eye on."

If your potential buyer won't come up past $975,000, you won't get a deal if you're arguing the position. You might, however, be able to solve the issue that satisfies your interest. For example, your agent could negotiate a lower price for the home you want, or show you a less expensive home that fits your wants and needs. Both of these solutions might allow you to accept the slightly lower offer on your home and still achieve your essentials.

Competition versus collaboration strategies

The two most common approaches to real estate negotiations are the competition and collaboration strategies.

The competition strategy argues for each party's positions. It's adversarial and assumes that for one side to win, the other must lose.

Competition tactics:

- Persistence, repeating arguments

- Abuse of power (short deadlines, bullying)

- Lowball/highball (anchoring the negotiation to an arbitrary low or high number)
- Create competition ("we're interested in two other units, so we don't really need this one" or "another party is coming for their second viewing later today")
- Manipulating facts/statistics

A collaborative strategy negotiates for interests, some of which the other party may share. Common tactics aim to explore both sides' wants and needs in order to find common ground – enabling both sides to win.

Collaboration tactics:

- Ask questions to understand needs
- Gather information
- Explore alternatives
- Generate positive emotions
- Build and extend trust

It may feel good to imagine your agent will use purely collaborative strategies. You get the price and the terms you want – and both sides win. However, real estate negotiations often require elements of both approaches. A high-level negotiator knows which tactics to use in different situations. Your agent, for example, could use competitive tactics within a collaborative strategy to elicit more favourable responses from the other party and help both sides reach an agreement.

The zone of agreement

In real estate, negotiating an offer means discovering whether we can reach a deal that satisfies both parties. If a homeowner is wed to their list price, even though the home has been on the market for over 200 days, there's likely no zone of agreement. Most buyers won't pay a price that the market has clearly proven is too high.

When a buyer believes, rightly or wrongly, that the market is shifting and prices are on their way down, and writes an offer 10 per cent below list price on a brand-new listing, there's likely no zone of agreement. Sellers don't generally accept such a low offer right out of the gate.

As agents, we're committed to getting the best price for our clients, but it has to make sense for the other side as well, or the deal won't happen. I've often heard it said that a successful negotiation means both sides agree to a price that doesn't make either of them particularly happy, but it's one they can both live with.

***

A negotiation gone wrong

Many years ago I helped a professional couple with two young children to buy their first home. They had an accepted offer on a three-bedroom townhome, steps from the seawall in downtown Vancouver. The property was in an older building that had completed an exterior remediation, but some deferred maintenance remained. My clients were keen to learn more by reading the strata documents in conjunction with their inspection report.

On the last day of the subject period, my clients decided to move forward with the purchase, but they wanted to negotiate a price reduction to account for the upcoming expenses of an anticipated capital project. We wrote an addendum to lower the price by $35,000, which the seller countered. By 7 pm, after a few rounds of back and forth, we were $5,000 apart. The negotiation hit a standstill. Neither side would move forward, so our contract expired that night.

The next morning, my client called me about a rare house on a small Kitsilano lot that had just come on the market. She noted that saving the monthly strata fee would make this well-priced house affordable for them. if it looked good in person, they wanted to make an offer. In fact, they were so keen, they asked me to arrange for both a showing and a home inspection that very day. We viewed the vacant home at 11am and they loved it. The inspector arrived by noon, and they wrote a subject-free offer as soon as he finished. By 6pm that night, they had bought the house.

Just before 7pm, my phone rang. It was the listing realtor from the townhome. "My seller is ready to give the extra $5,000," he said. The realtor was gobsmacked when I told him that my clients had already bought another property. His clients lost a deal worth over $1.2 million dollars for a difference of just $5,000.

It's worth repeating: your position and motivation give your realtor their negotiating power. That's why their tactics are constantly changing. Expert negotiators don't always beat up the other side and win at all costs. They might, if that's what you want them to do, but you also need to understand the risks of this approach – namely, that you might lose the deal.

Sometimes, you don't need to win the lowest possible price; you want to secure the property at a justifiable price. How we negotiate on your behalf depends on your motivations, your back-up plan, and how much you love a property. It also depends whether the market favours buyers or sellers, and which side we're on. It depends on what we know about the other party and their motivations and what we know about the realtor on the other side of the transaction. When we negotiate, our job is to find a zone of agreement – and to give you the opportunity to buy or sell the home within that zone.

CHAPTER 17:
AFTER THE CONTRACT

Once you have a firm offer on your sale or purchase, you're in the final stretch of this exhilarating process. It's common for both buyers and sellers to feel two related emotions in the days after the deal:

- **That's it?** Buying and selling have taken up so much of my life for two months – and now it's over?

- **Buyer's remorse**. Did I buy the right house? Did I pay too much? Did I sell for too little? Why did I sell my home at all? I love this house!

All of these thoughts and feelings are normal. You've made some big decisions, and as prepared as you were throughout the process, negotiations can happen very quickly. You might feel like your head is spinning. According to most estimates, one in five buyers and sellers have some regrets in the days after they close a deal. Acknowledge your feelings, remember why you wanted to make a move, talk to a trusted friend, or share your thoughts with your agent. These doubts usually don't last long, and you can work through the temporary discomfort together.

A story of buyer's remorse

I worked with a family with two small kids that was ready to move from their condo to a townhome or half duplex. They chose to sell first, because they knew they'd be buying at the top of their budget and couldn't risk a slow sale or selling their home for anything less than top dollar.

We sold their home well, negotiated for a long completion, and moved on to the buying process. The search for their new home took some time. There was one good choice early on, but it wasn't quite right and it sold to another buyer. We offered on another home, in competition, and another party came to the table with guns blazing and beat us on price.

About two weeks after we sold their condo, the mom came to me in tears. She was scared they wouldn't be able to find a new home before they had to vacate their condo, and asked me to get them out of the deal. Of course there was little chance their buyer would have changed their mind in the last two weeks, but I immediately called the agent and asked anyway. I listened to my client, acknowledged her understandable fears, and tried to reassure her that we still had lots of time. We would find the right one.

Sure enough, a spacious duplex on an oversized lot in their preferred neighbourhood came up just a few days later and we bought it for them. They lived there happily for several years before we sold the duplex and bought them a character home on a corner lot in East Vancouver.

Once the deal is finalized, your agent will walk you through the last steps:

- Ensure your lender has everything they need
- Choose a legal professional to manage the conveyance
- Complete any outstanding tasks (per the sales contract), such as removing a light fixture, repairing nail holes, removing plant pots from the yard, and more
- Inform utility companies of your upcoming move

- Call your insurance company

- Explore moving companies

- Clean the home you've sold

- Arrange to meet your agent at your new property on possession date, or drop off the keys to the home you've sold

You'll speak to your agent far less during this period than you have to date, but they're still there for you if you have questions or just want to run an idea by them. They would love to hear from you right up to possession date – and anytime after that, too. Your realtor can provide referrals to contractors and service providers, check in on your property value if the need arises, and even offer design ideas.

You should always feel free to contact your agent with any questions or concerns you have about your home, even years later. The rapport and trust you've built should continue through to the next time you plan to buy or sell again (or you refer a friend or family member). The best agents consider their client relationships to be far more than transactional. They want to stay in touch and help you however they can.

CHAPTER 18:
WRAP-UP – AND CONGRATULATIONS

You've now done something most consumers never will: you've learned the basics about how real estate is bought and sold, and how you can partner with your realtor to enjoy the best possible experience and results.

This knowledge will be powerful when you interview realtors to determine who can most effectively meet your needs, rather than hiring based on personality or convenience. You know some of the strategies, services, and skills they need to get the job done. You'll find that competence, professionalism, skill, and service are appealing qualities, and your trust and connection will build throughout the process.

You'll enjoy weighing in on buying or selling strategies with your realtor. You'll feel more confident and less anxious, because you understand the choices they're making – and why. You won't be as daunted by the work you have to do, because you know its purpose, and you have a partner to help you.

During the negotiation process, you won't be afraid to share the information your agent needs to negotiate for your interests, and not just your positions, so you can strike a deal that satisfies your wants and needs.

Knowing what great real estate agents and teams do empowers you to hire one and work effectively alongside them. When you're an active partner in the process, you'll enjoy the experience more, and achieve better results. Those results could include a higher sale price for your home, a better choice for your new home, or a more seamless process – whatever is most important to you.

Lastly, thank you.

Throughout my real estate career, I've strived to become the full-service, skilled, ethical agent I've described throughout this book. I thought it was enough to offer that commitment to my clients, with the help of my well-trained and talented team, but it feels good to share this information with you.

My sincere hope is that you now have more context and confidence to advocate for yourself and participate fully in your real estate journey. There are many dedicated professionals working in real estate who will be an excellent partner for you, and together, you can achieve so much.

www.ingramcontent.com/pod-product-compliance
Lightning Source LLC
LaVergne TN
LVHW020716060325
805263LV00008B/69